JEAN JOHNSON

THREADS & TIES THAT BIND

Exquisite Quilts from Tie Fabrics

THE QUILT DIGEST PRESS
Simply the Best from NTC Publishing Group
Lincolnwood, Illinois U.S.A.

746.46
JOH

Editorial and production direction by Anne Knudsen.

Cover design by Karen Christoffersen.

Text design by Kajun Graphics, San Francisco.

Book editing by Karen Steib.

Technical editing by Kandy Petersen.

Technical drawings by Kandy Petersen.

Photography by Sharon Risedorph, San Francisco.

Printed in Hong Kong

BS

Library of Congress Cataloging-in-Publication Data

Johnson, Jean.

      Threads and ties that bind: exquisite quilts from tie fabrics/Jean Johnson.

           p.   cm.

      ISBN 0-8442-2625-4

      1. Patchwork—Patterns. 2. Quilting—Patterns. 3. Patchwork quilts.

          I. Title

TT835.J584 1996

746.46'041—dc20   96-3057

                                               CIP

Published by The Quilt Digest Press

a division of NTC/Contemporary Publishing Company

4255 West Touhy Avenue

Lincolnwood (Chicago), Illinois 60646-1975, U.S.A.

©1997 by Jean Johnson. All rights reserved.

No part of this book may be reproduced, stored in a retrieval system,

or transmitted in any form or by any means, electronic,

mechanical, photocopying, recording or otherwise, without the prior

permission of NTC/Contemporary Publishing Company.

Contents

Introduction

*Q*uilters are always planning their next quilt—always thinking of new designs and materials. This book shows you how to put a new spin on quilting by using the gorgeous fabric from men's ties. Go through your husband's or son's closet, pick out the ties he no longer wears, choose a pattern you like, and follow the instructions provided in these pages to create a one-of-a-kind quilt that is not only beautiful but distinctly personal.

Tie fabrics are usually extraordinary: soft and supple materials, wonderful rich textures, and intricate designs. Few people can afford to spend $45 to $65 a yard for quilt fabrics, but ties provide the means of using exquisite silks to create masterpieces. The fabrics can be prepared so they are perfect for quilting, and there are many advantages to using these materials. They are easy to work with and long lasting, and they hold their color perfectly. The choice of design is endless, and the colors range from pale to bold with every gradation in between.

This is your chance to be truly creative. Whether you choose a simple pattern like MILKY WAY or the more complex DOUBLE WEDDING RING, no two quilts will be alike because no one will have the same collection of ties. And with each collection comes a different set of memories and meanings. For instance, I had a friend who used her husband's ties to make a quilt while mourning his passing. The project helped her through the healing process. Not only did it give her something tangible to keep, but it allowed her to reflect on their lives and work through her grief.

A quilt is a statement in fabric. It tells people a lot about you without you saying a word. In this book, you will find many old favorites, patterns that have lasted for generations and were probably used by your grandmother. You can use these classic patterns to create any kind of quilt you choose—the only limitation is your own imagination. You can make a quilt with fabrics from one color family, as I did with the vivid burgundies in DRESDEN PLATE, the deep golds in DAHLIA, or the blues in OCEAN WAVES. Ties come in so many colors and designs, the possibilities are endless.

Every time I make a quilt with ties, I'm amazed at how easy it is. It is perfect for the beginner, but equally challenging for the experienced quilter. So read through the chapters, choose your favorite pattern, and begin making your quilt of memories today.

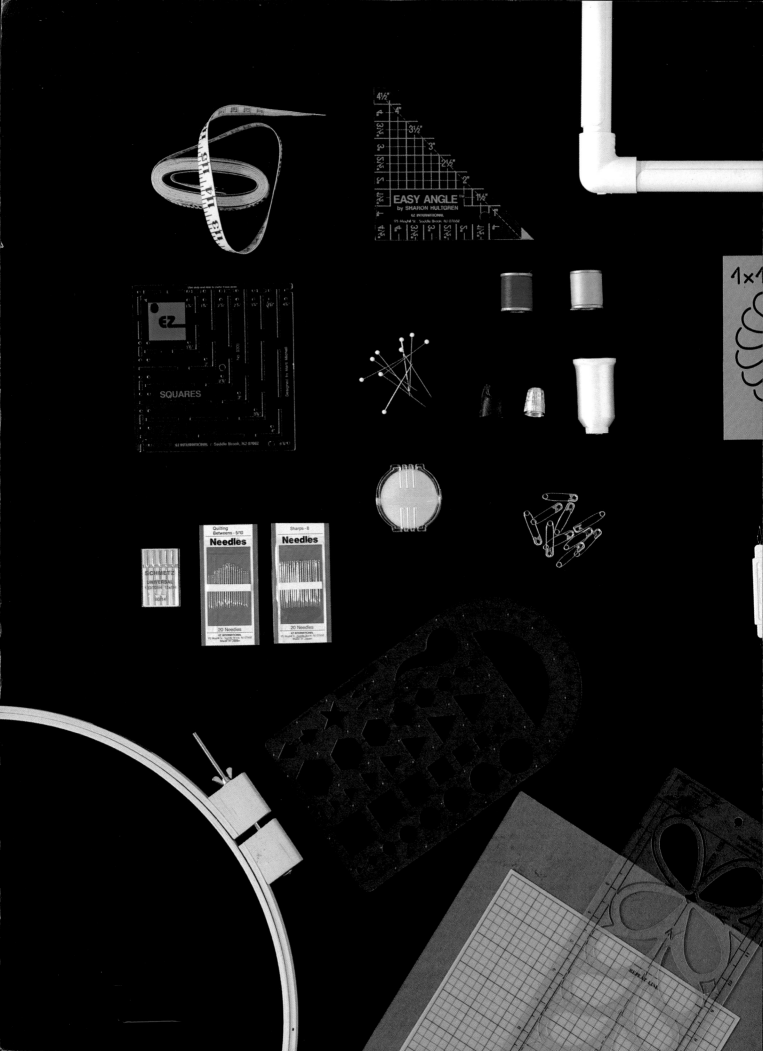

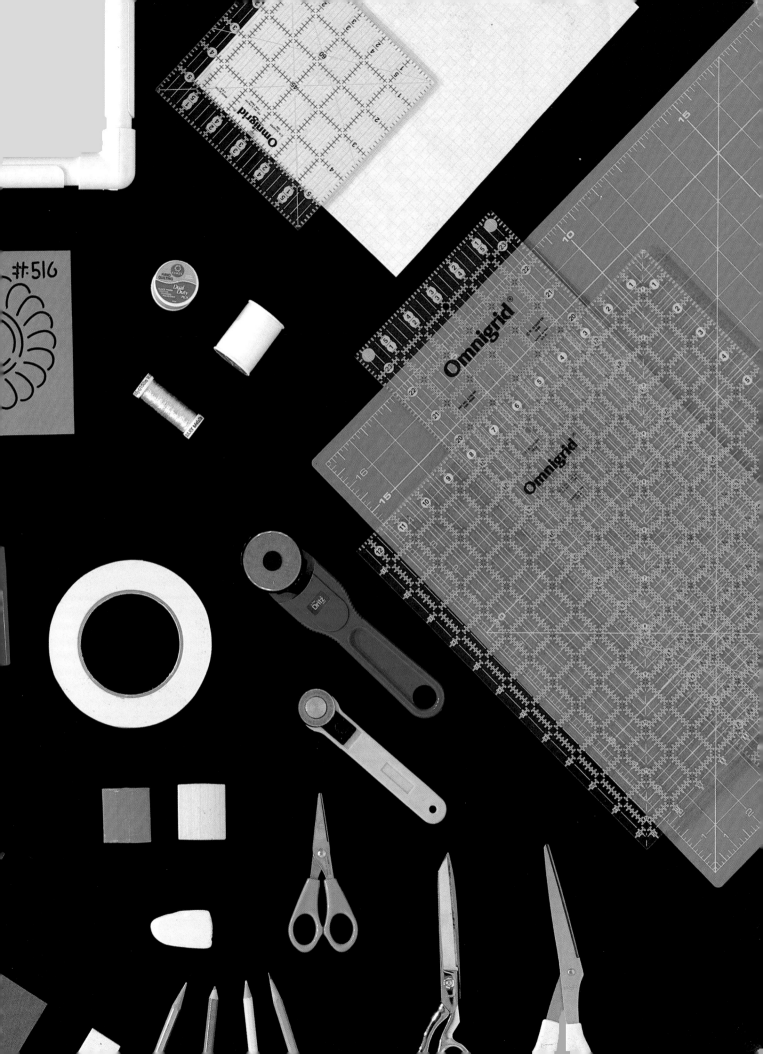

Materials and Supplies

*I*f you sew, you probably already have the tools you need for quilt making. If you need to purchase special tools, buy the best you can afford, and be sure to take care of all tools regularly. Sharpen shears and scissors; change rotary cutting blades or have them sharpened as they begin to dull; discard dull needles and bent or dull pins. Keeping your tools in good condition will make quilting a breeze and help you turn out a more professional-looking product.

Cutting Tools

Rotary cutting mat — Used with a rotary cutter; 17″ x 23″ is the best size for most cutting jobs.

Rotary cutting rulers (6″ x 24″; 6″ x 6″; and 12½″ x 12½″) — Thick, clear acrylic rulers with markings for length, width, and 45- and 60-degree angles.

Rotary cutters (one large, one small) — Used with a cutting mat and a rotary cutting ruler for quick cutting and for trimming pieces or blocks to proper size. The blades are retractable for safety.

Fabric shears — Used for cutting fabric for times when a rotary cutter is inappropriate.

Paper scissors — Used for cutting paper, plastic, and other materials that would dull good fabric shears.

Small scissors — Used for clipping threads.

Marking Tools

Choose the marker that works best with whatever fabric you're using. Try them on a scrap of material before using them for quilt pieces.

Silver quilter's pencil

Yellow quilter's pencil

Clean erase quilting pencil

#2½ lead pencil

Permanent marker (fine point) — Used to sign quilts or mark templates. This should always be tested on a scrap of fabric before using to be sure it won't bleed.

Tailor's chalk

Soap sliver — A small piece of white soap that makes a clear mark and is easy to remove.

¼″ (64mm) masking tape ∽ Used to make a perfect ¼″ (64mm) seam or evenly spaced quilting lines.

White fabric eraser ∽ Used to remove pencil marks from fabrics. *Never use colored erasers.*

Sewing Tools

Sewing machine ∽ Any straightstitch machine that makes even stitches will work.

Hand sewing needles (sharps) ∽ Used for general purpose sewing. The smaller the needle, the finer the stitches.

Darning needles ∽ Long, thin needles that can be used to baste the three layers of the quilt together.

Sewing-machine needles ∽ Should be needles made for woven fabric in a size 10 to 14 (universal size 70 to 90).

Glass head pins (1¾″)

Pin cushion

#1 steel safety pins ∽ Used for pin basting quilts.

#1 curved basting pins ∽ Easier than regular steel safety pins to insert through three layers of fabric.

Metal thimble

Leather thimble

Machine or hand sewing thread

Invisible nylon monofilament thread ∽ Often used on the top of the sewing machine for attaching appliqués. It blends with any fabric and comes in clear for light colors and smoke for darker colors.

Fusible thread ∽ Usually used in the bobbin. This allows you to press a hem or binding in place for hand sewing without pinning or basting.

Beeswax in holder ∽ Strengthens thread and helps prevent kinking and knotting when hand sewing.

Seam ripper ∽ Used to remove a machine-sewn seam. When the point is used to cut every fourth or fifth stitch, the thread on the opposite side will unravel.

Needle threader

Little foot ∽ A sewing machine foot that stitches an exact ¼″ (64mm) seam.

Mitering tool ∽ Shaped for marking sewing lines to make a perfectly mitered corner.

Scrap saver ∽ Used when trimming a square composed of two triangles.

Measuring Tools

120″ tape measure ∼ Ideal length for quilting. This will measure the largest king-size quilt.

Easy angle ∼ Used to cut triangles from a strip of fabric and to trim triangles after sewing.

Squares ∼ Helps cut or trim squares up to 4½″ (11.5cm).

Pressing Equipment

Iron

Ironing surface ∼ A small and a large ironing board are both useful.

Quilting Supplies

Batting ∼ Used as the middle layer of the quilt.

Wooden quilting hoop ∼ A large hoop that holds material taut for lap quilting. A 14″ to 18″ (30.8cm to 41cm) hoop is the best size.

Plastic-pipe quilting frame ∼ Also used for lap quilting. Each of the four sides has a clamp that allows material to be tightened as needed.

Quilting design templates ∼ Available in many designs and sizes.

Quilting thread ∼ A strong, heavy thread that comes in a variety of colors and will not twist or kink easily.

Metallic thread ∼ Used for Christmas or other projects where a touch of glitter is desired. Use no more than 18″ (41cm) of thread at a time when quilting.

Betweens quilting needles ∼ Short, strong needles. The higher the number on the needle, the smaller the needle. Beginners may wish to use a size 8 or 9, with size 12 being the smallest.

Template-Making Tools

Graph paper. Used for drafting patterns or for drawing and coloring block layouts. Use a good-quality, ¼″ (64mm)-grid graph paper; a ½″ (1.2cm)-grid may be used for coloring designs.

Protractor ∼ An all-purpose tool that helps you draw several sizes of circles, squares, and triangles, as well as angles.

Plain template plastic ∼ Used for curved templates.

Gridded template plastic ∼ Used for straight-line templates.

Freezer paper ∼ Used for templates that will adhere to fabric, thus creating a sewing line without marking.

How to Use This Book

In this book you will find:

- Illustrations of 13 exquisite quilts made from tie fabrics
- Step-by-step instructions on how to make each quilt
- Clear, easy-to-follow diagrams to show exactly how the quilt is made
- Accurate templates
- Ideas for varying the patterns to give your quilts a one-of-a-kind look

In addition, this book explains key skills in quilt making that will make it easier for you to work with tie fabrics:

- Finding and collecting tie fabrics to create your own tie library
- Preparing ties for quilting
- Using freezer-paper templates to make it easier to cut silky tie fabrics
- Making borders with perfectly mitered corners
- Choosing batting
- Quilt assembly, including making backings and bindings

The quilts selected for this book are traditional designs. Your old favorites are all here—GRANDMOTHER'S FLOWER GARDEN, DOUBLE WEDDING RING, DRESDEN PLATE, and many more. All use simple straight- or curved-line quilting designs, easily mastered by the novice quilter. The quilts are presented in order of difficulty. Beginners can learn new techniques as they work through the book, while more experienced quilters can sharpen their skills and try something new. There are also ideas for variations on each quilt so the more adventurous can try out more complex color and fabric combinations or use more elaborate quilting designs to create special one-of-a-kind quilts.

Using tie fabrics in quilting presents a few challenges. First, you have a limited amount of fabric from each tie, making the placement of templates for minimum waste especially important. Second, because you will be working with small pieces of fabric, patterns with large templates are more difficult to handle. Third, many ties have very elaborate designs that require special consideration when placing templates so patterns match in the final product.

The rewards of working with the rich, high-quality materials used for ties more than makes up for the extra effort. All tie fabrics are different, and even simple stripes present new opportunities for experimenting and re-arranging. You can use the intricate designs on many ties to create special effects. There is a real sense of accomplishment in discovering how to put together two small pieces of fabric to produce a unique design, as I did with the center squares of MILKY WAY.

It is both exciting and satisfying to work with so many beautiful fabrics to create extraordinary quilts that have special meaning and memories. Each quilt will be a work of art. As you work with ties, you will find new ways to express yourself and find ways to build on the patterns and suggestions provided in this book. *Threads & Ties That Bind* challenges your creativity and opens the door to a whole new world of quilt making.

Jean Johnson

Getting Started

*O*nce you have read through *Threads & Ties That Bind* and have chosen a pattern for your first tie quilt, you'll be ready to begin. Several quilt-making processes are used again and again, no matter what quilt you decide to work on. These processes are explained in this section and referenced as needed in specific chapters. You will also find the answers to some of the most frequently asked questions about quilting with ties, as well as helpful hints to guide you through the basics and more advanced techniques.

Is Working with Tie Fabric Different Than Working with Other Fabrics?

Yes. Tie fabric is not a set width or length as regular yardage is. It also tends to be slippery and a bit more difficult to handle than most quilting fabrics, but you can counteract this by using freezer-paper templates or fusible interfacing.

Is the Whole Quilt Made with Ties?

Usually not. Other types of fabric are normally used as background blocks, sashing, borders, and backing.

Does It Matter How I Lay Out the Templates on the Fabric?

One straight edge of the template is usually placed on the straight grain line, as is true for any fabric. However, ties sometimes have designs that take precedence over the line of the grain.

Where Do I Find Tie Fabrics?

The simple answer is that you create your own tie collection. A perfect place to start is with your family. Raid your husband's or son's closets and you're sure to uncover lost treasures. Old favorites, their colors delicately faded with use. Christmas and birthday gifts with beautiful, multicolored fabrics that were not, perhaps, quite to the receiver's taste and have hung forlorn ever since the packages were opened. Wide ties—great for cutting larger pieces—that are long since out of style. Ties for special occasions in silks and fancy jacquards, holiday ties, ties from Father's Days or birthdays, or ties with cartoon characters on them.

Next, call on relatives. Your father or grandfather, particularly if he is retired, is sure to have a stash of work ties he no longer needs. Because they were worn by close family members, these ties have special meanings, making them all the more precious to work with. The quilt you make will bring back happy moments and sad and will be treasured all the more for the memories woven into it.

Ask friends, too, to help you broaden your collection. Most will be relieved to find a purpose for the ties that languish in their closets! Check out thrift shops, church rummage sales, and flea markets. Sometimes, you'll find ties made from wonderful antique fabrics that hold their colors and shapes through generations. They are a pleasure to quilt with—and so easy! You'll soon find that you have hundreds of ties, many new and no two alike.

Tie scraps are often available from tie factories. Your local library should have a list of addresses and telephone numbers. Call to find out whether factories will give you scraps or sell ties with flaws.

How Do I Prepare the Ties for Quilting?

Ties are usually made from very high-quality fabrics, which means they wear well and are very durable. They are also completely washable. However, before you start using ties in quilts, you will need to do the following:

1. Sort the ties into those that are made with natural fibers and those with man-made fibers. The manufacturer's tab, sewn into the narrow end of the tie, usually indicates material. Natural fibers include silk, wool, linen, and cotton. Man-made fibers include polyester, polyester and cotton blends, and acetate.
2. Sort each fiber group by color and shade.
3. Rip the ties apart, taking care not to cut or snag the fabric. Discard the interfacings and linings, and remove all loose threads.
4. Wash the ties one at a time in warm, sudsy water. Wash the lightest ties first and check for color fastness. If a tie colors the water, set it aside and wash it again in fresh water. If it continues to bleed after three washings, do not use it in a quilt. Rinse each tie thoroughly.
5. Roll the ties in terylene towels to absorb most of the moisture or put them in a lingerie bag and damp-dry them in the dryer.
6. Iron, wrong side up, until completely dry.

The tie fabrics are now clean, pressed, and ready to use in quilts. Store them in boxes that are clearly labeled with the color and fabric content. Flat shirt boxes work well; plastic boxes are not recommended. If you have many ties in one color family, you might want to divide them into light, medium, and dark categories.

⁓Keep a diary as you quilt so your children and grandchildren, too, can share the memories. Note who each tie in your quilt belonged to and tell any special stories you remember about them.

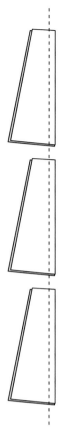

Diagram 1

What Sewing Methods Will I Use?

A quilt may be sewn by machine or by hand.

HAND PIECING

Hand piecing involves making tiny stitches on the seam line. Seams are pressed in one direction, not pressed open.

ENGLISH PAPER PIECING

This is a method of sewing pieces together for a perfect fit that is difficult to achieve by machine.

1. Baste each piece to a paper template, folding the seam allowance over the edge of the template. Press.
2. Pick up the two pieces, right sides together. Using a whipstitch, join the pieces, catching only the folded edges. Press. Remove the bastings and paper templates.

MACHINE PIECING

Quicker than hand piecing, in machine piecing two pieces are placed right sides together and machine stitched from edge to edge. Backstitching is not necessary.

CHAIN STITCHING

Chain stitching is a fast method of machine sewing pairs of pieces together, one after another, without breaking the thread connecting them (see Diagram 1). Cut the pairs apart when sewing is complete.

What Are Freezer-Paper Templates and Why Should I Use Them?

It is difficult to mark cutting and sewing lines on tie fabric. Freezer-paper templates—meaning template shapes that have been cut from freezer paper—provide an easy alternative. When the freezer paper is pressed to the tie fabric with a warm iron, it adheres to the fabric. You can then cut around the template, leaving a $1/4''$ (64mm) seam allowance. You can buy freezer paper in the paper goods section of any grocery store. Look for the regular weight since the heavy-duty paper is more difficult to use.

I like freezer-paper templates and always recommend them for beginners. Although it takes time to trace the templates onto paper and cut them all out, in the long run, using them helps you avoid cutting and sewing mistakes and minimizes wasted fabric. Freezer-paper templates are also reliable—they stay exactly where you put them and are an excellent guide not only for cutting but for sewing lines.

To make and use freezer-paper templates, follow these guidelines:

1. Trace the templates onto the dull side of the freezer paper. Do not

add seam allowances, as the edge of the template itself will serve as your sewing line.

2. Cut out the required number of each template and stack them waxy side down.
3. Press the freezer-paper templates onto the wrong side of the fabric using a warm, dry iron to help them adhere.
4. Remove the templates when the quilt top is complete.

How Do I Use Fusible Interfacing?

⁓Some interfacings carry the label "low temperature". They work on both light- and heavyweight fabrics, and are equally useful for silk or polyester ties. Set your iron to the silk setting when using these interfacings.

Fusible interfacing used with light or slippery fabrics helps stabilize the fabric, making it easier to sew and quilt.

1. Using a rotary cutter, cut interfacing pieces to fit each template piece that requires this treatment. Do not add $\frac{1}{4}$" (64mm) seam allowance as you do with fabric pieces. Label and store the pieces until just before you are ready to cut your fabric.
2. Before fusing interfacing to template fabric, test it on a scrap, using the least amount of time listed on the package for a firm fuse. Remember that fusing to polyester may take less time than noted on the package directions.
3. During the first few seconds of pressing the interfacing onto the fabric, wiggle the iron to prevent bumps from the iron steam vents.

How Do I Make the Quilt Borders?

A border is not only a frame for the quilt as a whole, but is an integral part of the design. You may have one border or multiple borders of varying widths. Take as much time planning the border as you do the quilt. Make all of the blocks and take them to the fabric store to try them next to different materials. The right choice will be obvious.

With all of the quilts in this book, you can use either tie fabric or other selected fabric for the border. If you decide to use tie fabric, you will need to sew several pieces together into a long strip. For a 2" (5.1cm) border, cut left-over pieces from your ties into bars $2\frac{1}{2}$" (13.1cm) wide to allow for the seams. Sew the bars together to make four borders, one for each side of your quilt. Make sure your final strips are 4" (10.2cm) longer than the sides of the quilt to allow enough fabric for mitering the corners.

Borders with Perfect Mitered Corners

A mitered corner is formed when the horizontal and vertical borders are joined at 45-degree angles. If more than one border is used, sew the borders together and miter as though they were one piece of fabric. As one of the

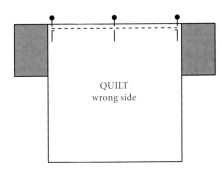

Diagram 2

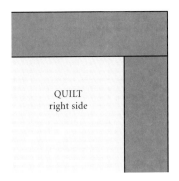

Diagram 3

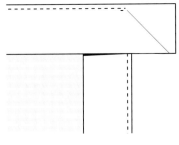

Diagram 4

finishing touches on your quilt, borders look especially pretty if the corners are mitered perfectly. If you have not mitered a corner before, practice with an 8″ (20.3cm) square of fabric and two strips measuring 3″ x 12″ (7.6cm x 30.5cm).

1. Align the right side of the first border with the right side of the quilt, leaving equal amounts of border extending at each end. Pin in the center and then out to the ends, as shown in Diagram 2.
2. Begin sewing ¼″ (64mm) from the edge of the quilt. Backstitch. Sew to the opposite end, stopping at the seam allowance. Backstitch.
3. Add the other three borders in the same way, taking care not to stitch through the previously sewn borders. A right angle will form at each corner.
4. Turn the quilt right side up and press the borders away from the quilt.
5. Trim the border extensions, using neighboring borders as a guide. (See Diagram 3.)
6. Align the border extensions, right sides touching. Make sure the corners are square.
7. Draw a diagonal line from the outside corner to the backstitching point. Pin. (See Diagram 4.)
8. Begin sewing at the backstitching point, following the drawn line to the corner.
9. Trim to a ¼″ (64mm) seam.
10. Miter all four corners and press the seams.

How Do I Know What Type of Batting to Use?

If you have ever shopped in a large specialty quilt store, you know how difficult it can be to choose batting. If you haven't, you'll be amazed at how many types of batting are available. Batting is available in traditional, low-loft, hi-loft, ultra-loft, and extra-loft varieties, and names vary with the manufacturer. The type of batting you choose depends on how much quilting you want to do. Since the batting can totally change a project, each type giving your quilt a different look and feel, it is important to take care in making your selection. Read the package labels for quilting distances.

Batting thicknesses range from ⅛″ to 2″ (32mm to 5.1cm). The thinner the batt, the smaller the quilting stitches can be. Batting comes in sizes big enough for a king-size quilt (120″ x 120″ [305cm]) and small enough for a crib (45″ x 60″ [114cm x 152cm]). It also comes by the yard in 45″ (114cm), 54″ (137cm), and 90″ (229cm) widths. There are basically three types: *needlepunch*, where the fibers are tangled together; *glazed*, where resin is sprayed on both sides; and *heat,* where the edges are sealed.

Batting is available in polyester, cotton, wool, and polyester blends.

Cotton

Cotton works best in small projects, clothing, and thin quilts. It is cool in summer and warm in winter. It softens with use, giving your quilt a cozy, worn-in feel. Smaller stitches are possible with cotton batting than with any other kind, and it works equally well with either hand or machine quilting.

The downside of cotton batting is that it can shrink, losing up to 5″ (12.7cm) in a king-size quilt. Quilting also can be a little more difficult than with other battings, as the natural fibers are not always even. For the same reason, it needs to be quilted more closely than other battings.

Wool

Like cotton, wool batting is breathable, provides warmth, and is completely washable. Moths will not eat through the cotton fabric surrounding the batting as long as it is kept clean.

The disadvantage of wool batting is that much of it beards (tiny fibers creep through the quilt top, giving a lint-like appearance), and this is especially noticeable on dark fabrics. There is, however, at least one wool batt made with the needlepunch method that will not beard. Again, check the package label before you buy.

Polyester

Polyester works well with any size quilt and is readily available in a variety of dimensions. Because it is very washable, it is recommended for bed quilts that are in constant use. Polyester batting is lightweight, and most good brands have an even thickness. This means that quilting does not have to be as close together as with cotton or wool batting.

However, quilting can be more difficult with polyester than with batting made from natural fibers. Bearding can occur as you quilt—stitching brings the fibers through the front of the quilt. Even though polyester washes well, the thickness, or loft, of the batting tends to get lower with every wash.

Before you use any type of batting, remove it from its packing, spread it out flat, and let it rest overnight. Most of the folds and wrinkles will disappear. If necessary, lightly tumble dry for 10 to 20 minutes to remove any remaining wrinkles.

If you use a lot of batting, keep records on index cards stapled to the batting to remind you of the brand name, fiber content, closeness of quilting needed, and any other relevant information.

⌢ Some quilt and fabric stores will let you use their large tables for preparing your quilt.

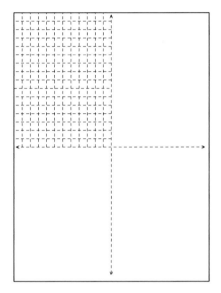

Diagram 5

How Do I Assemble My Quilt?

Once your quilt top is made, give it a final pressing to prepare it for layering with batting and backing. Mark the quilting lines if you are using a design other than straight lines that can be marked with masking tape.

Adding the Backing and Batting

Choose a good-quality cotton fabric for the backing—it is much easier to quilt and will not slide off the bed. Be sure the design will not show through to the front of the quilt. Choose a solid color that will complement the colors in the quilt top if you want the quilting stitches to show on the back. Choose a patterned fabric if you don't want the stitches to show as much. Do not use a sheet: It is too tightly woven to quilt well.

1. Cut out the backing fabric to the length indicated in the quilt pattern you are using. Usually you will need at least two or three lengths of fabric. Trim the selvages.
2. Sew the lengths together with ¼″ (64mm) seams. Press the seams open.
3. Lay out the backing, wrong side up. If you can, tape it to a table, stretching the fabric slightly. Lay on the batting, then the quilt top, right side up.
4. Baste, using Diagram 5 as a guide. Start in the center of the quilt and baste to the outer edge, dividing the quilt into quarters. Baste about 2″ (5.1cm) to 3″ (7.6cm) apart in each quarter.

Edging the Quilt

Once you have finished quilting the body of the quilt but before you quilt the border, finish the edges as explained below. Edging is particularly important with tie fabrics, as it prevents silky materials from slipping when the binding is sewn in place.

1. Using chalk or a soap sliver, draw a line around the outside of the border where the binding will be sewn and pin the edge.
2. Sew around the quilt along the outside of the line. Trim close to the sewing line.
3. Machine overcast around the outside edge of the quilt, covering the line of stitching.

The border is now ready for quilting.

Binding

A binding is a piece of fabric that is used to finish the edge of the quilt. I prefer to use a folded strip of binding, creating a two-layer piece of fabric that encases the quilt edge for a more durable finish. Bindings can be made

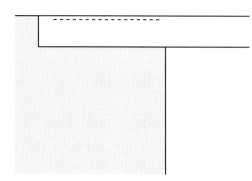

Diagram 6

from the same fabric as the outside border or from one of the fabrics used in the quilt. A binding should be cut on the straight grain for a quilt with straight sides and on the bias for a quilt with a curved edge.

1. Sew the binding strips into one piece, long enough to go around the entire quilt.
2. Fold and press the binding in half lengthwise.
3. Starting 8″ (20.3cm) to 10″ (25.4cm) from the corner on the front of the quilt, pin the raw edge of the binding to the edge of the quilt.
4. Using a ¼″ (64mm) seam allowance, begin sewing 1″ (2.5cm) from the beginning of the binding. Backstitch. Sew to the ¼″ (64mm) seam allowance on the opposite end. Backstitch. Cut the thread. (See Diagram 6.)
5. Fold the binding and pin to the side of the quilt, as in Diagram 7. Sew this side, beginning at the edge of the quilt and stopping ¼″ (64mm) from the opposite end. Cut the thread.
6. Repeat steps 3 to 5 until the binding is sewn onto all sides of the quilt. Trim off excess binding, leaving a 1½″ (1.3cm) overlap at each end.
7. Fold the binding over to the back edge of the quilt just covering the stitching and pin in place. Fold the next side over and pin, mitering the corners.
8. Blind stitch the binding to the backing and slipstitch the mitered corners.
9. Remove the bastings.

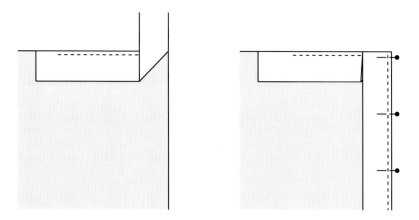

Diagram 7

Fusible thread can be used in the bobbin when sewing on the binding. Simply sew the binding to the quilt, then fold it to the back of the quilt and press in place before hand sewing.

Finishing the Quilt without Using a Binding

An alternative to binding a quilt is to finish the outside edge with a narrow hem by folding the front edge of the quilt to the back and sewing it in place. This method can be used when you want a simple, smooth finish that carries the border color over the edge of the quilt without the extra seam of an added binding. Quilt all but the final border, finish the edging, and complete the quilting.

1. Fold the edge of the quilt under by ¼″ (64mm) and baste. (Do not baste through the backing and batting.)
2. Trim the batting and backing to ⅜″ (86mm) shorter than the edge of the basted border. Turn the basted edge to the back of the quilt and pin in place. Hand sew all four sides. Remove bastings.

THREADS
&
TIES THAT
BIND

Milky Way

64″ x 80″ (163cm x 203cm)

This quilt uses an elaborately designed silk tie fabric in a soft shade of brown, with a Jacquard yellow contrast fabric. The border is made from tie fabric and the binding is made from the contrast fabric.

Milky Way

$\mathcal{M}$ILKY WAY is a classic quilt design that dates back as early as the 1870s. A favorite among Indiana's pioneer settlers in the 1920s, it is also known as Indiana Puzzle. The design has been found in quilts honoring political leaders and has even been used for the border of a medallion quilt with an astronomy theme. Perhaps it is the quilt's geometrically fascinating lines that explain its popularity and its appeal in such unusual quilts.

MILKY WAY is deceptive in its simplicity. Based around a simple nine-block pattern, it is one of the easiest classic quilts to make. It is ideal for beginners because it is traditionally made from just two colors. It is a good opportunity to work with the simplest of color schemes and to practice using light and shade. The bold pattern that characterizes MILKY WAY means that the quilt can easily adapt to a variety of sizes, from a miniature quilt with tiny half-inch (1.2cm) squares to dramatic five-inch (5.1cm) squares on a king-size quilt.

Choosing Fabrics

The quilt shown is made in just two colors from silk scraps found in a tie factory. As you can see from Diagram 1, the pattern is ideal for making from ties because each of the blocks is pieced together from small cuts of fabric. The only difficulty is the larger center-square piece in Section A, which, as we shall see, can easily be pieced together from smaller cuts and trimmed.

Block Construction

As shown in Diagram 1, the block comprises three sections. Section A is a simple nine-patch made up of nine 4″ (10.2cm) squares (excluding seam allowances). Section B is a rectangle using three 4″ (10.2cm) squares; Section C uses four 4″ (10.2cm) squares. When the three sections are sewn together, the finished size of the block is 16″ by 16″ (40.6cm), plus ¼″ (64mm) seam allowances. The number of blocks that you use will determine the size of your quilt.

Partial Section C is Section C from which template A has been omitted. This is necessary to complete the final vertical row of the quilt. Use Diagram 2 and the chart below as a guide to the number of blocks you will need to make MILKY WAY in the size you choose. An optional 2″ (5.1cm) border of tie or contrast fabric can be added.

Block A   Block B

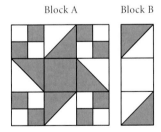

Block C

Diagram 1

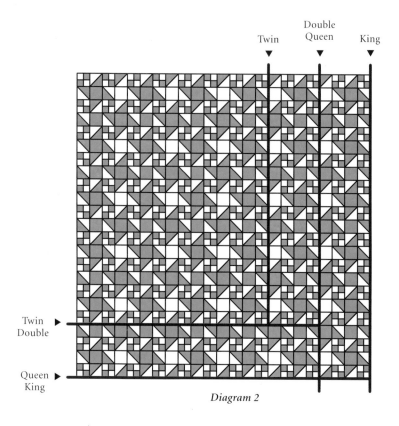

Diagram 2

	TWIN 64″ × 80″ (163cm × 203Cm)	DOUBLE 80″ × 80″ (203cm × 203cm)	QUEEN 80″ × 96″ (203cm × 244cm)	KING 96″ × 96″ (244cm × 244cm)
Section A	20	25	30	36
Section B	15	20	24	30
Section C	15	20	24	30
Partial Section C	5	5	6	6

Fabric Requirements

MILKY WAY uses almost equal amounts of tie fabric and contrast fabric. The quilt shown uses elaborately designed tie fabric in a soft shade of brown, against a yellow jacquard fabric.

Tie Fabric ⌒ *Number of templates needed*

	TWIN	DOUBLE	QUEEN	KING
Center squares *(template A)*	32	41	50	61
Small squares *(template B)*	160	200	240	288
Triangles *(template C)*	142	180	218	264

Contrast Fabric

	TWIN	DOUBLE	QUEEN	KING
Center squares (template A)	31	40	49	60
Small squares (template B)	160	200	240	288
Triangles (template C)	142	180	218	264
Binding—2½″ (6.4cm wide)	305″ (7.75m)	340″ (8.64m)	370″ 99.40m)	400″ (10.16m)
Total amount of fabric needed	3 yds (2.74m)	3¾ yds (3.43m)	4½ yds (4.12m)	5 yds (4.57m)

	TWIN	DOUBLE	QUEEN	KING
Short mitered border—cut 2	2½″ × 68″ (6.4cm x 172.7cm)	2½″ × 84″ (6.4cm x 213.4cm)	2½″ × 84″ (6.4cm x 213.4cm)	2½″ × 100″ (6.4cm × 254cm)
Long mitered border—cut 2	2½″ × 84″ (6.4cm × 213.4cm)	2½″ × 84″ (6.4cm × 213.4cm)	2½″ × 100″ (6.4cm × 254cm)	2½″ × 100″ (6.4cm × 254cm)
Total amount of fabric needed	3½ yds (3.2m)	4 yds (3.66m)	5 yds (4.57m)	5½ yds (5.03m)

Other

	TWIN	DOUBLE	QUEEN	KING
Backing	5 yds (4.57m)	5 yds (4.57m)	6 yds (5.49m)	9 yds (8.23m)

Cutting the Fabric

⁓ If you do not have enough large pieces of tie fabric to cut out the center squares (template A), sew two triangles of tie fabric together and trim to the 4½″ (11.4cm) square needed. The effect can be quite beautiful.

1. Using templates A, B, and C and following the charts above, cut out the required number of pieces from the tie fabric. Freezer-paper templates work well with silks and can be used if desired (see page xv). Stack the pieces in groups of Section A, Section B, and Section C.
2. Trim the selvages from the contrast fabric.
3. Using the contrast fabric, cut two 2½″ (6.4cm) strips of binding along the entire length of the fabric. Cut a third strip long enough to total the amount needed for the size quilt you are making. (Cutting the long pieces first allows for as few seams in the binding as possible.)
4. Using templates A, B, and C and following the charts above, cut out all pieces from the contrast fabric. Stack the pieces in groups of Section A, Section B, and Section C.

Making the Quilt Top

⁓ To make seams match perfectly, push the pin through the meeting point of the seam on one piece and then into the meeting point of the seam on the second piece. Make sure the pin goes straight through both strips.

1. Pin all small squares (template B) into pairs side by side, one of each color. Pin all triangles (template C) across the angle to create squares, using one triangle of each color.

⤳ When machine sewing light and dark silky fabrics together, match the thread to the darker fabric. Use a fine needle and high-quality thread.

⤳ If you take care to press the seams correctly, the three rows will sew together with much less bulk at the seams. Press the seams of the top and bottom strips toward the center square. Press the seams of the center strip away from the center square.

2. Sew together the pairs of small squares from edge to edge. Match with a second pair of small squares, reversing the colors as in Diagram 3, and sew the two pairs together to create a larger square made up of four units.

3. Sew together the pairs of triangles. Note that the seam is on the bias; take care not to stretch the fabric.

4. Using a rotary cutter and a square ruler, trim each of the pieces into an exact 4½″ (11.4cm) square.

5. Lay out Section A using Diagram 3 as a guide.

6. Sew together the three units that make up the top, center, and bottom strips. Press the seams.

7. Pin, sew, and press the three rows together into a nine-patch, as in Diagram 4.

8. Lay out the vertical Sections B and the horizontal Section C as shown in Diagram 1. Pin and sew together the three units that make up each of the two strips.

9. As shown in Diagram 5, pin and sew Section B then Section C to the nine-patch. Press. This completes the MILKY WAY block.

10. Pin and sew the rows together to form a complete quilt top. If you used freezer-paper templates, remove them now.

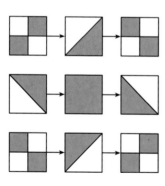

Diagram 3

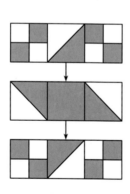

Diagram 4

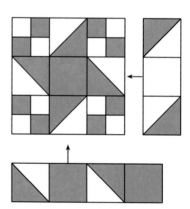

Diagram 5

Making the Border

The border of the quilt shown is made from pieces of the tie fabric sewn together into a long strip. The border can just as easily be made from the contrast fabric. Cut four strips of fabric 2½″ (6.4cm) wide to fit the length and width of the quilt top. Allow an extra 4″ (10.2cm) for each border in order to miter the corners. Follow the instructions for assembling the border and mitering the corners on page xvi.

Notice that for some of the diagonals you can quilt in long lines across the entire quilt.

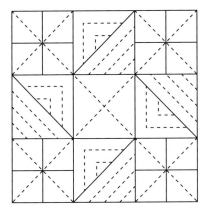

Diagram 6

Quilting

Prepare your quilt for quilting by adding the backing and batting, following the instructions on page xix.

In the quilt shown, several styles of quilting are used, as indicated in Diagram 6.

1. The center squares and the four-patch squares are quilted corner to corner.
2. The tie-fabric triangles are quilted with three rows of evenly spaced lines.
3. The contrast-fabric triangles are quilted with two lines, each forming a half-square pattern.

Finishing the Quilt

Finish the edge of the quilt following the guidelines on page xix. Quilt the border as desired. Make and sew on the binding following the instructions on page xxi.

Variations

Though the quilt shown uses just two colors, MILKY WAY can be made in any number of more complex color and cloth combinations. Try experimenting with color by tracing the design onto graph paper and coloring as you wish. If you decide to use more than two colors, use Diagram 2 to calculate the number of pieces of each template in each color you will need.

When using more than two colors, I prefer to keep the contrast color the same throughout the quilt. A pretty way to use many colors is to make each diagonal row of tie fabrics a different color, giving a rainbow effect. Solid colors would be striking in this instance. Of course, each block can also be made from a different tie to create a scrap effect.

MILKY WAY is ready for you to use and dream of sleeping under the stars.

Grandmother's Fan

61½" x 88½" (156cm x 225cm)

The eight blades in each fan are made from tie fabrics. Tans and browns in all shades and designs are accented by one or two shades of green. The taupe background and the forest green border are made from non-tie fabrics.

Grandmother's Fan

*G*RANDMOTHER'S FAN is a romantic quilt pattern dating from the last quarter of the nineteenth century. Graceful and elegant, the pattern is thought to have derived from Japanese designs in the 1890s. Reaching the height of its popularity during the Victorian era, the pattern appears both in the elaborately embroidered quilts of that period and in simple scrap quilts using pastels from the depression years of the 1920s and 1930s.

GRANDMOTHER'S FAN is easy to make, yet allows for endless variety. The pattern is ideal for practicing machine piecing and appliqué techniques.

Choosing Fabrics

The shape of the blades in GRANDMOTHER'S FAN make it ideal for working with ties. Allowing a mix of designs and colors, bright, shiny tie fabrics bring an elegance to the quilt that is reminiscent of Victorian days. Color choices can be as wide-ranging as your collection of tie fabrics allows. You can use different colors and shades for every blade. The key is to experiment until you find a color scheme that works. Lay out the thin ends of your ties together and move them around until you are pleased with the results.

Use a background fabric that compliments the ties. If your ties are light and bright, consider a black background for the striking effect of diamonds, rubies, and emeralds playing on black velvet. If your ties are darker, use a light or medium background fabric. For the border, sashings, and backing, try matching the color to one of the strongest tie fabrics.

Block Construction

Each block consists of a fan of tie fabrics appliquéed to a background block. The finished sizes include 1½″ (3.8cm) sashing, a 1½″ (3.8cm) border made from sashing fabric, and a 3″ (7.6cm) border made from background fabric. No binding is used. Instead, the border is folded over ½″ (1.3cm) to the back.Use the chart below to determine the number of blocks you will need.

	TWIN 61½″ × 88½″ (156cm × 225cm)	DOUBLE 75″ × 88½″ (191cm × 225cm)	QUEEN 88½″ × 88½″ (225cm ×225cm)	KING 102″ × 102″ (259cm × 259cm)
Block size	12″ × 12″ (30.5cm)	12″ × 12″ (30.5m)	12″ × 12″ (30.5cm)	12″ × 12″ (30.5cm)
Rows	4 × 6	5 × 6	6 × 6	7 × 7

Fabric Requirements

GRANDMOTHER'S FAN uses ties to make the eight fan blades—six from shades of tan to brown and two from greens. The quilt shown has a silky taupe fabric for the block background and outside border. To accent the greens in the fans, a silky forest green fabric is used for the sashing and first border. The backing is a forest-green print.

Tie Fabric ∼ Number of templates needed

	TWIN	DOUBLE	QUEEN	KING
Fan blades (template A)	192	240	288	392

Background Fabric

	TWIN	DOUBLE	QUEEN	KING
Blocks 13″ × 13″ (33cm)	24	30	36	49
Fan handles (template B)	24	30	36	49
Short border—cut 2	4″ x 56″ (10.2cm × 142.2cm)	4″ × 69½″ (10.2cm × 176.5cm)	4″ × 83″ (10.2cm × 210.8cm)	4″ × 96½″ (10.2cm × 245.1cm)
Long border—cut 2	4″ × 90″ (10.2cm × 228.6cm)	4″ × 90″ (10.2cm × 228.6cm)	4″ × 90″ (10.2cm × 228.6cm)	4″ × 103½″ 10.2cm × 262.9cm)
Total amount of fabric needed	4 yds (3.66m)	5 yds (4.57m)	5¾ yds (5.26m)	7¾ yds (7.09m)

Contrast Fabric

	TWIN	DOUBLE	QUEEN	KING
Short sashing strips 2″ x 13″ (5.1cm x 31.8cm)	20	25	30	42
Long sashing strips	3 (2″ × 80″) (5.1cm × 203.2cm)	4 (2″ × 80″) (5.1cm × 203.2cm)	5 (2″ × 80″) (5.1cm × 203.2cm)	6 (2″ × 93½″) (5.1cm × 237.5cm)
Short border—cut 2	2″ × 53″ (5.1cm × 134.6cm)	2″ × 66½″ (5.1cm × 168.9cm)	2″ × 80″ (5.1cm × 203.2cm)	2″ × 93½″ (5.1cm × 237.5cm)
Long border—cut 2	2″ × 83″ (5.1cm × 210.8cm)	2″ × 83″ (5.1cm × 210.8cm)	2″ × 83″ (5.1cm × 210.8cm)	2″ × 96½″ (5.1cm × 245.1cm)
Total amount of fabric needed	3 yds (2.74m)	3 yds (2.74m)	3 yds (2.74m)	4 yds (3.66m)

Other

	TWIN	DOUBLE	QUEEN	KING
Backing	5¼ yds (4.8m)	5¼ yds (4.8m)	5¼ yds (4.8m)	8¾ yds (8m)
Sheer interfacing	2 yds (1.83m)	2¼ yds (2.06m)	2½ yds (2.29m)	3 yds (2.74m)

You can also stabilize the fabric by using a sheer fusible interfacing before cutting out the pieces.

Cutting the Fabric

1. Using template A and following the charts above, cut out the required number of pieces from the tie fabric. Freezer-paper templates work well because the blades have bias edges and the freezer paper will hold the fabric without stretching (see page xv). Stack the blades according to the tie fabric used.

2. From the background fabric, cut the long borders first, then the short borders. Next cut out the background squares. Finally, using template B, cut out the fan handles.

3. From the contrast fabric, first cut the long borders and the long sashing pieces. Next, cut the short borders and the short sashing pieces.

Making the Blocks

1. Lay out eight blades for each block. Experiment until the arrangement pleases you. Try alternating light or medium blades with dark ones. In the quilt shown, no more than one blade from each tie fabric is used in a single block. At least two blades in an accent color are used in each block.

2. Turn the blades wrong-side up, keeping the same arrangement. Label the eight blades in the first block as blades 1(a) to 1(h), the blades in the second block as blades 2(a) to 2(h), and so on.

3. Pin 1(a) to 1(b), 1(c) to 1(d), 1(e) to 1(f), and 1(g) to 1(h). Do the same for each block. Chain sew together all the pairs of blades (see page xv for an explanation of chain sewing).

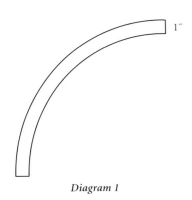

Diagram 1

4. Stack the pairs that make up each block together. Press the seams.

5. Pin and sew two pairs of blades together, as in step 3 above, trim, and press.

6. Pin and sew the two halves of each fan together and press.

7. Create a template for the interfacing by tracing the long, outer edge of the fan to a depth of approximately one inch (see Diagram 1). Using sheer sew-in interfacing, cut a piece to face each fan in the quilt top.

Facing the outer edge of the fan with a sheer sew-in interfacing provides for a smooth curved edge that is much easier to sew than raw tie fabric. The facing does not need to be fused in place.

8. Lay the facing onto the right side of each fan, pin in place, and sew a ¼" (64mm) seam along the long edge. Understitch the edge of the facing. Turn the facing to the wrong side of the fabric and press from the right side.

9. Using template B and sheer interfacing, make a facing for each fan handle. Sew the facings to the fabric handles. Pin a handle to each fan and sew in place. The fans are now complete.

10. Mark each background block to show the position of the fan and fan handle, as shown in Diagram 2.

Facings are understitched to keep them from showing on the right side of the quilt top. With the fan right side up, pull the facing and seam to the side and stitch on the facing near the seam line (through both the facing and the seam). The interfacing will fall into place.

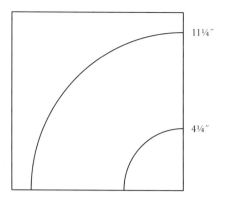

11¼″

4¼″

Diagram 2

◞ *Use a long thin needle to appliqué the fan onto the background square. Cotton (100%) is the best choice of thread. It doesn't tangle as easily as polyester or polyester blends.*

11. Pin the fan in place, taking care that there are no wrinkles in the background fabric. Hand appliqué.

12. Cut away the background fabric from under the fan. Square and trim each block to 12½″ x 12½″ (31.8cm).

Making the Quilt Top

Diagram 3 shows just three different ways of laying out the blocks; many more are possible, depending upon the quilt size you are making. Remember to allow for 1½″ (3.8cm) sashing between the blocks.

1. Number the blocks as shown in Diagram 4.

2. Pin and sew the short, horizontal sashing strips to the bottom of each of blocks 1, 2, 3, 4, and 5. (Since this is where the border goes, there is no need for sashing at the top of block 1 or at the bottom of block 6.)

3. Create rows of blocks by sewing each block to the horizontal sashing. Press.

4. Pin and sew the long, vertical sashing strips to connect the vertical rows. Connect row 1 to row 2, row 3 to row 4, then, finally, row 2 to row 3. Press.

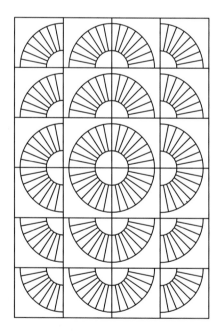

All sizes
Diagram 3a

Twin or queen only
Diagram 3b

Twin or queen only
Diagram 3c

Row 1	Row 2	Row 3	Row 4
1	7	13	19
2	8	14	20
3	9	15	21
4	10	16	22
5	11	17	23
6	12	18	24

Diagram 4

Diagram 5

Making the Borders

There are two borders on the quilt shown. The inner border, made from the same fabric as the sashing, is 1½″ (3.8cm) wide. The outer border, made from the background fabric, is 3½″ (8.9cm) wide.

1. Make the inner border by sewing the two short border strips to the top and bottom of the quilt top. Press the seams toward the border fabric. Next, sew the long border strips to each side of the quilt top. Press.

2. Attach the outer border in the same way. Press.

Quilting

Prepare your quilt for quilting by adding the backing and batting, following the instructions on page xix.

1. Quilt in the ditch (in the seam line) around the sashing and around the long and short curves of the fan.

2. Quilt the rest of the block as shown in Diagram 5. The echo quilting lines (the multiple lines of quilting that follow the fan shape) are ¾″ (1.9cm) apart.

3. Quilt the sashing and the inner border using 1″ (2.5cm) diagonal squares, as shown in Diagram 5.

Finishing the Quilt

Finish the edge of the quilt without using a binding by following the guidelines on page xxi. Quilt the outside border with three rows of quilting: one row in the middle of the border and one on either side.

Variations

Although the fan blades face the center of the quilt shown here, there are many other ways to place the blocks. Try moving them around to form other designs.

For a Victorian look, add lace around the outer edge of the fan and around the handle, add bows at the base of the handle, and/or add pretty buttons 1″ (2.5cm) apart down each fan blade.

Alternatively, you may choose to add embroidery stitches over the sewing lines where the fan blades are sewn together.

GRANDMOTHER'S FAN is now ready to become your own family heirloom.

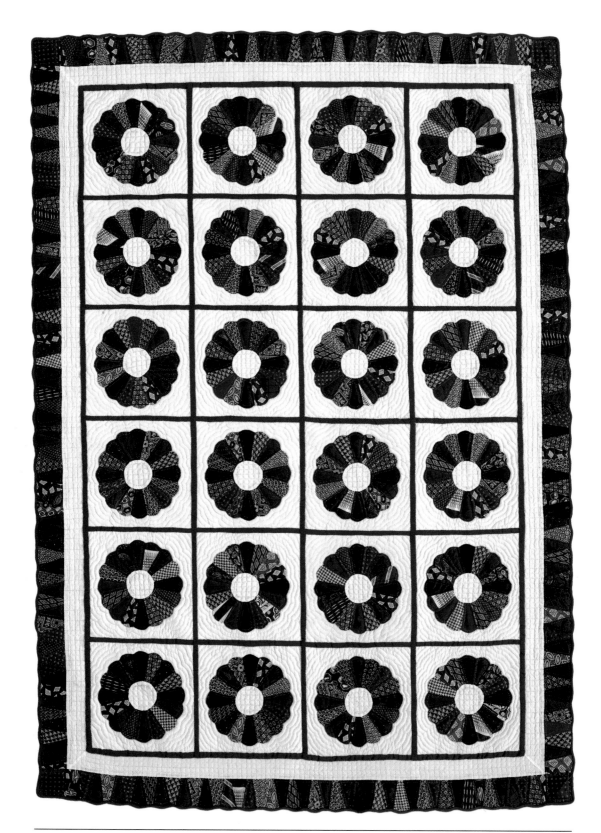

Dresden Plate

62½″ × 88″ (159cm × 224cm)

A combination of tie fabrics in varying hues of burgundy solids and designs is used for the plates and border on this quilt. The rich color scheme is highlighted by a white background and echoed in the burgundy fabric used for the sashing, narrow border, and binding.

Dresden Plate

The traditional DRESDEN PLATE pattern was probably first made in the nineteenth century, although a variation of it appeared in a Bride's Quilt by Anna Tuel in 1785. The name derives from the Dresden china factory, which manufactured the first true porcelain in Europe in the early 1700s. This china was highly prized in nineteenth-century American homes, becoming a symbol of elegance and good taste for many prairie wives.

DRESDEN PLATE not only makes a beautiful quilt; it is popular with less-experienced quilters for its simple design. Also known as Sunflower, Bride's Quilt, Aster, and Friendship Ring, this versatile pattern allows for a wide range of colors and color combinations.

Choosing Fabrics

DRESDEN PLATE patterns of the 1920s and 1930s were usually made in pastel colors, but bright, shiny tie fabrics make a cheerful, vibrant quilt. Look through your tie collection as you decide what color scheme you want to use. In the quilt shown here, all plates are in shades of one color. One tie fabric is repeated in several of the plates. Choose at least 16 ties, more if desired, from one color family. Other color options are given at the end of the chapter, under Variations.

Block Construction

The finished size for this quilt includes ½″ (1.3cm) sashing, a 2″ (5.1cm) border in background fabric, and a 4″ (10.2cm) plate border with a narrow binding. All blocks are 12″ × 12″ (30.5cm). Use the chart below to determine the number of blocks you will need.

	TWIN 62½″ × 88″ (159cm × 224cm)	DOUBLE 75″ × 88″ (191cm × 224cm)	QUEEN 88″ × 100″ (224cm × 254cm)	KING 100″ × 100″ (254cm × 254cm)
Rows of blocks	4 × 6	5 × 6	6 × 7	7 × 7

Fabric Requirements

DRESDEN PLATE uses ties for the 16 wedges of each plate, all from shades of one color. The quilt shown uses a white background and center circles, with burgundy sashing and binding.

It is difficult to give an exact number of ties needed for a quilt because of the variety of tie sizes. It is always best to lay the templates out on a tie you are considering to see how far the material will go.

Tie Fabric ∼ Number of templates needed

	TWIN	DOUBLE	QUEEN	KING
Plate wedges *(template A)*	384	480	672	784
Curved border wedges *(template A)*	110	120	138	148
Straight border wedges *(template C)*	106	116	134	144
Half straight border wedges *(half template C)*	8	8	8	8
Corner squares for wedgeborder *(template D)*	4	4	4	4

Background Fabric

	TWIN	DOUBLE	QUEEN	KING
Plate blocks—13″ × 13″ (33cm × 33cm)	24	30	42	49
Short mitered border—*cut 2*	2½″ × 58″ (6.4cm × 147.3cm)	2½″ × 71″ (6.4cm × 180.3cm)	2½″ × 83″ (6.4cm × 210.8cm)	2½″ × 96″ (6.4cm × 243.8cm)
Long mitered border—*cut 2*	2½″ × 83″ (6.4cm × 210.8cm)	2½″ × 83″ (6.4cm × 210.8cm)	2½″ × 96″ (6.4cm × 243.8cm)	2½″ × 96″ (6.4cm × 243.8cm)
Center circles *(template B)*	24	30	42	49
Total fabric needed	4½ yds (4.11m)	5½ yds (5.03m)	6¾ yds (6.17m)	7¾ yds (7.09m)

Contrast Fabric

	TWIN	DOUBLE	QUEEN	KING
Short sashing strips— 1″ × 12½″ (2.5cm × 31.8cm)	20	25	36	42
Long sashing strips	3 1″ × 75″ (2.5cm × 191cm)	4 1″ × 75″ (2.5cm × 191cm)	5 1″ × 87½″ (2.5cm × 222.3cm)	6 1″ × 87½″ (2.5 × 222.3cm)
Short border (2)	1″ × 50″ (2.5 × 127cm)	1″ × 62½″ (2.5cm × 158.8cm)	1″ × 75″ (2.5cm × 191cm)	1″ × 87½″ (2.5cm × 222.3cm)
Long border (2)	1″ × 76″ (2.5cm × 193cm)	1″ × 76″ (2.5cm × 193cm)	1″ × 88½″ (2.5cm × 224.8cm)	1″ × 88½″ (2.5cm × 224.8cm)
Binding—2″ (5.1cm) wide	325″ (825cm)	350″ (889cm)	400″ (1016cm)	425″ (1080cm)
Total fabric needed	3 yds (2.74m)	3 yds (2.74m)	3½ yds (3.2m)	3½ yds (3.2cm)

Other

	TWIN	DOUBLE	QUEEN	KING
Backing (cotton fabric)	5½ yds (5.03m)	5½ yds (5.03m)	9 yds (8.23m)	9 yds (8.23m)

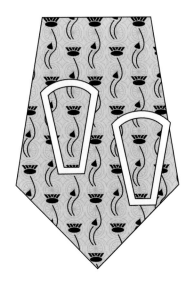

Diagram 1

Cutting

Freezer-paper templates (see page xv) work well for this pattern, providing both a sewing guide and a guide for folding under the outside edges of the plates accurately.

Tie-Fabric Plates

Using the templates and following the charts above, cut out the required number of pieces from the tie fabric. If a tie has a design you want to appear the same on each plate wedge, make a window template using template A.

1. Place the tie right side up and lay the window template on it, adjusting it until the design you like appears in the window (see Diagram 1). Place a freezer-paper template in the window.

2. Remove the window template and press the freezer paper in place.

3. Repeat for each piece as necessary, then cut out all templates, allowing for a ¼″ (64mm) seam.

4. Peel the freezer-paper template off and press it on the wrong side of the plate wedge.

⁓ It is a good idea to make a sample plate out of scraps before using your tie fabric. Be sure to lay scrap pieces on your chart to test your template size for accuracy. If each wedge is as little as ¹⁄₁₆″ (3mm) off, your plate may be 1″ (1.3cm) larger or smaller than planned, meaning it will not lay flat and the center circle will not fit

Dresden Plate Border

1. For every six plate wedges you cut from each tie, cut one curved wedge (template A) and one straight wedge (template C) for the border.

2. Cut four freezer-paper template Cs in half. Press all eight pieces on one tie, leaving a ¼″ (64mm) seam allowance on all sides. Cut out. These pieces will be placed on either side of the four corner plate border squares (see Diagram 2).

3. Cut four corner squares (template D) from one tie.

Background Fabric

Cut out the long borders first, the short borders next, then the background blocks, and last the plate centers (template B).

Contrast Fabric

Cut the required pieces in the following order:

1. Long border and long sashing pieces

2. Bias binding strips (see Diagram 3)

3. Short border and short sashing pieces

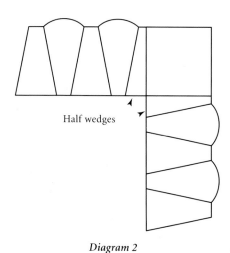

Half wedges

Diagram 2

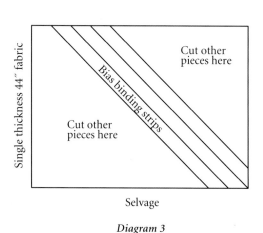

Single thickness 44″ fabric

Cut other pieces here

Bias binding strips

Cut other pieces here

Selvage

Diagram 3

Making the Quilt Top

1. Lay out the plate wedges (template A) for each block. Number Block 1 wedges 1-1, 1-2, and so on, in order around the plate. Repeat for each plate.

2. Working with one plate at a time, pin and sew wedge 1 to wedge 2, wedge 3 to wedge 4, and so on around the plate. Begin sewing at the dot

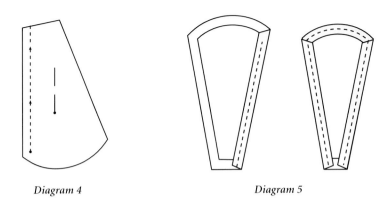

Diagram 4   *Diagram 5*

at the top of template A, and continue off the opposite end, as in Diagram 4. Press seams in one direction. Your plates should lie flat.

3. Turn under the curved edge, keepingthe edges even, and baste. Press.

4. If you are using the English paper piecing method (page xv), construct plates as shown in Diagram 5. Press.

5. To make each center circle, run a basting thread in the seam allowance around the freezer-paper template. Pull the thread tightly until it forms a perfect circle and knot the thread. Press from the top. Pin the center in place, checking from the back to be sure it is centered and all edges of the plate are caught under the circle. Hand sew around the circle and press. Repeat for all plates.

6. Fold the background fabric in half vertically, then horizontally, and crease lightly. Reopen and place the plates on the background using the creases as a guide (see Diagram 6). Align a seam on each plate with a crease on the background square, pin in place and hand sew around the outside of the plate. Repeat for all plates.

7. Remove all basting and, from the back, cut out the background fabric about ⅜″ (1cm) inside the sewing line where the plate is attached (see Diagram 7), and square each block to exactly 12½″ × 12½″ (31.8cm), keeping the plate centered.

8. Lay out all your blocks and arrange them as desired.

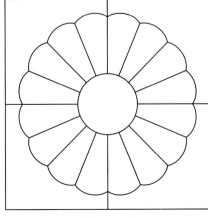

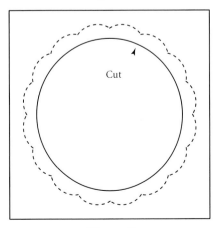

Diagram 6   *Diagram 7*

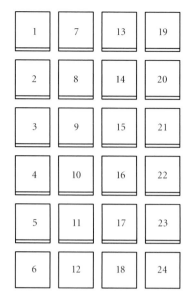

Diagram 8

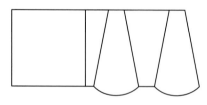

Diagram 9

9. To add ½" (1.3cm) sashing between blocks, sew a short piece of sashing to the bottom of blocks 1 through 5 in Row 1, blocks 7 through 11 in Row 2, and so on for all the rows in your quilt (see Diagram 8).

10. Connect all the blocks in Row 1. Repeat for the remaining rows. Press all seams toward the sashing.

11. Pin and sew long sashing strips between the rows to form the quilt top. Be careful not to stretch the sashing. Press the seams toward the sashing.

Making the Borders

1. Sew the short narrow borders to the short wide borders. Sew the long narrow borders to the long wide borders. Use each as a single border. Press.

2. Attach the borders, mitering the corners, following the instructions on page xviii.

3. To make the DRESDEN PLATE border, take out your border pieces and arrange them in order. Chain sew the border, alternating templates A and C, as in Diagram 9. Continue sewing until you have a strip that fits each side of your quilt. Press all the seams in one direction. Sew one half of template C on each end of all four border pieces. Press. Sew one corner square to each end of the other long border pieces (see Diagram 9). Attach the short borders to the top and bottom of the quilt and the long borders to the sides. Press.

Quilting

Prepare your quilt for quilting by adding the backing and batting, following the instructions on page xix.

1. Quilt ¼" (64mm) from the edge on the inside of all plate wedges, around the outside of the plate, and in ½" (1.3cm) squares in the center circle.

2. Quilt in the ditch (seam line) around the sashing and the narrow border. Echo quilt the background (see Diagram 10). *Do not quilt the wide border yet.*

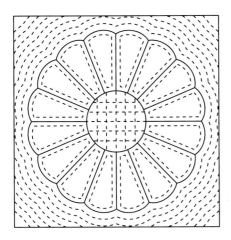

Diagram 10

Finishing the Quilt

1. Sew together the bias binding you cut earlier into one long strip. Fold it in half, and press.

2. Lay the binding on the top of the plate border and carefully sew around the curves of the border. Trim the seam as necessary. Turn the facing to the back and hand sew.

3. Quilt the outside border in ½″ (1.3cm) squares to match the center circles. Quilt the DRESDEN PLATE border the same way you quilted the plates.

4. Remove the basting stitches.

Variations

1. As stated earlier in the chapter, there are a variety of color schemes you may choose from for this pattern:

   - All plates alike with every wedge in the plate different. This option only works for twin- and double-size quilts. To make each plate the same, you must be able to cut one wedge for each plate from one tie and no more than 30 wedges can be cut from even the largest tie. Choose 16 ties that look nice when arranged in a circle. For this design, a solid-color border is used—you may choose the same fabric you use for the center circles. If you use tie fabric for the center circles, another contrasting fabric can be used for the border.

   - All plates different, with each plate using two colors. You will need one tie that has two distinct designs or colors in it for each block. The ties must be large enough to allow for eight wedges on each color. Alternatively, you could choose two ties with patterns that blend well for each block, in which case you will need only eight wedges from each tie. A solid border looks best with this color scheme.

   - All plates different. This will give a scrap-quilt effect. Choose ties of various colors that look great together.

2. If you do not want to add the DRESDEN PLATE border, make and sew on the binding following the instructions on page xx. Quilt the wide border in ½″ (1.3cm) squares.

   This is a quilt you will enjoy looking at as much as you enjoy using it.

Dahlia

56″ × 71″ (142cm × 180cm)

The flowers in this quilt are made up of tie fabrics in various shades of green and gold with a few other colors mixed in. Contrast is provided by the parchment and gold fabrics used for the background, nine-patch squares, sashing, border, and binding.

Dahlia

$\mathcal{D}$AHLIA is a very simple pattern which was popular in the early half of the twentieth century. It was usually made of dress calico in small pastel prints and light solids. A blanket stitch was often embroidered around the center circle and each petal to accent the classic lines of the design, and the quilt was almost always laid out with a solid-color sashing.

This is a perfect design for beginners because it is easy to make and the finished quilt is strikingly beautiful when made with bright, gleaming tie fabrics.

Choosing Fabrics

The tie fabric is normally chosen first. In this case, I saw the parchment and gold fabrics I wanted for the background and contrast fabrics and then decided to use ties in the gold and green color families.

If you want to make a traditional-looking quilt, choose ties that are light to medium in color. They should have small designs to resemble calico. Flowers made from this type of fabric may be accented with black blanket-stitch embroidery to give the quilt an antique look. (The embroidery can be done by hand or with a machine-sewn blanket stitch.) Print fabric may be used as a contrast fabric for the border with a narrower solid border to add interest.

Block Construction

The finished quilt includes a 4″ (10.2cm) border of background fabric, 3″ (7.6cm) of triple sashing, a triple sashing border, and a narrow binding. Use the chart below to determine the number of blocks you will need.

	TWIN 56″ × 71″ (142.2cm × 180.3cm)	DOUBLE 71″ × 86″ (180.3cm × 218.4cm)	QUEEN 86″ × 101″ (218.4cm × 256.5cm)	KING 101″ × 101″ (256.5cm × 256.5cm)
Block size	12″ × 12″ (30.5cm × 30.5cm)	12″ × 12″ (30.5cm × 30.5cm)	12″ × 12″ (30.5cm × 30.5cm)	12″ × 12″ (30.5cm × 30.5cm)
Rows	3 × 4	4 × 5	5 × 6	6 × 6
Nine-patch corner units	20	30	42	49

Fabric Requirements

I chose to use only two fabrics in addition to the ties. Because DAHLIA is so simple, I use a more elaborate setting, using the background and contrast fabrics in a three-strip sashing unit and a nine-patch corner unit to connect the sashing. This same design is used as a border, with a second border of background fabric and a narrow gold binding to finish the quilt. I stabilized all pieces in this quilt except the binding with a sheer fusible interfacing (see page xvi) because the fabric was very soft. The interfacing pieces were cut without seam allowances.

Tie Fabric ～ *Number of templates needed*

	TWIN	DOUBLE	QUEEN	KING
Flower petals (*template A*)	72	120	180	216
Flower centers (*template B*)	12	20	30	36

Background Fabric

	TWIN	DOUBLE	QUEEN	KING
Blocks 13″ × 13″ (33cm)	12	20	30	36
Sashing strips 12½″ (3.8cm × 31.8cm)	31	49	71	84
Strips for corner unit squares 1½″ × 15″ (3.8cm × 38.1cm)	10	15	21	25
Short mitered border	4½″ × 60″ (11.4cm × 152.4cm)	4½″ × 75″ (11.4cm × 191cm)	4½″ × 90″ (11.4cm × 228.6cm)	4½″ × 105″ (11.4cm × 266.7cm)
Long mitered border	4½″ × 75″ (11.4cm × 191cm)	4½″ × 90″ (11.4cm × 228.6cm)	4½″ × 105″ (11.4cm × 266.7cm)	4½″ × 105″ (11.4cm × 266.7cm)
Total fabric needed	3¾ yds (3.43m)	5¼ yds (4.8m)	6¾ yds (6.17)m	8¼ yds (7.54m)

Contrast Fabric

	TWIN	DOUBLE	QUEEN	KING
Sashing strips 1½″ × 12½″ (3.8cm × 31.8cm)	62	98	142	168
Strips for corner unit squares 1½″ × 15″ (3.8cm × 38.1cm)	8	12	17*	20*
Binding 2½″ (6.4cm) wide	265″ (6.73m)	325″ (8.26m)	385″ (9.78m)	415″ (10.54m)
Total fabric needed	2 yds (1.6m)	2¼ yds (2.06m)	3 yds (2.74m)	3¾ yds (3.43m)

You will have extra corner units.

	TWIN	DOUBLE	QUEEN	KING
Backing	4½ yds (4.11m)	5¼ yds (4.8m)	6 yds (5.49m)	9 yds (8.23m)
Sheer interfacing	13 yds (11.89m)	17 yds (15.54m)	21 yds (19.2m)	26 yds (23.77m)

Add a ⅜″ (1cm) seam instead of a ¼″ (64mm) seam to template B. This will make it easier to get a smooth round circle. The excess fabric can be trimmed off after the circle is basted. Alternatively, you can line template B and use only the ¼″ (64mm) seam allowance.

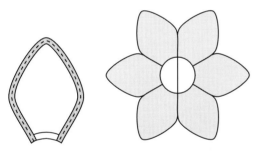

Diagram 1   Diagram 2

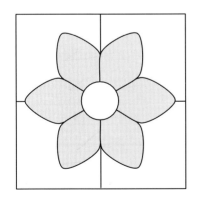

Diagram 3

Cutting

1. Using templates A and B and following the charts above, cut out the required number of pieces from the tie fabric. If you use freezer-paper templates (see page xv), draw a line across the petal template where machine or hand sewing should stop (see template A). You may want to use the English paper piecing method (see page xv) for this pattern as there is so little sewing to be done.

2. Following the guidelines on page xviii and the charts above, cut the interfacing for all pieces: outside border, sashing strips, nine-patch corner units, and background squares. Label and store these pieces until you are ready to cut your fabric.

3. Press the interfacing petals to the ties, keeping an eye on the tie designs. Press on the freezer-paper templates and cut out, leaving a ¼″ (64mm) seam allowance. Following the same procedure, prepare and cut out the background and contrast fabrics.

Making the Quilt Top

1. Baste under the edges of all petals except the curved center part (see Diagram 1).

2. To prepare the center circles, sew a gathering thread around the outside of the circle in the seam allowance. *Do not cut the thread.* Pull the gathering thread to make a perfect circle and knot the thread. Make all flower centers and press.

3. Place two petals right sides together and whip stitch up to the line across the template. Open up the petals and finger press. Add another petal, sew, and finger press. Continue until you have a complete flower. Repeat for each flower and press all of them from the right side.

4. Fold a flower center in half, creasing it lightly in the middle. Align the crease with the flower petal seams (see Diagram 2), pin, and hand sew in place. Press.

5. Fold each background block in half vertically, then horizontally, and crease lightly. Align the dahlia on the crease as in Diagram 3. Pin in place and hand sew. Cut the background fabric from under the flowers and remove the basting stitches. *Do not remove the freezer-paper templates.*

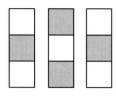

Diagram 4

6. Using the following charts, make the proper number of sashing strips, matching borders, and nine-patch corner units. Chain sew one contrast-fabric and one background-fabric strip for each sashing strip A needed. Cut them apart. Press seams toward the background-fabric strip. Attach another contrast-fabric strip to the other side of the background-fabric strip, and press the seams toward the center. Trim the two outside strips to exactly 1¼″ (3.2cm) wide.

	TWIN	DOUBLE	QUEEN	KING
Strip A—12½″ × 3½″ (31.8cm × 8.9cm) Contrast/Background/Contrast				
Sashing	17	31	49	60
Border	14	18	22	24
Strip B—15″ × 3½″ (38.1cm × 8.9cm) Contrast/Background/Contrast				
Sashing	13	24	40	50
Border	28	36	44	48
Strip C—15″ × 3½″ (38.1cm × 8.9cm) Contrast/Background/Contrast				
Sashing	6	12	20	25
Border	14	18	22	24

TWIN SIZE

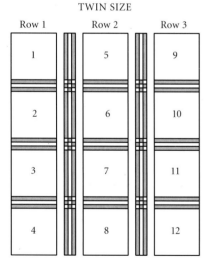

Diagram 5

7. Complete all of the sashing strips and border strips in the same way, following the order shown for Strip A above.

8. To assemble the nine-patch corner units, chain sew the three 15″ (38.1cm) strips together following the directions for Strip B and Strip C above, and press the seams toward the center strip. Cut all of strips B and C into 1½″ (3.8cm) strips. Lay out one nine-patch as in Diagram 4. Pin together the seam, sew, and press. Continue to chain sew the nine-patch blocks together and press.

9. Lay out all of the dahlia blocks and sashing, arranging as desired. Make a diagram for your quilt size following the sample in Diagram 5. Number the blocks according to your diagram.

10. Using the A sashing strips and the nine-patch corner units, connect the quilt top following Diagram 5. Press.

Diagram 6

Diagram 7

Making the Border

1. Following Diagram 6, make the short sashing borders and attach them to the top and bottom of the quilt top. Repeat for the long sashing borders and attach to the quilt sides.

2. Pin and attach the four outside border sections to each side of the quilt top, mitering the corners (see page xvi). Press.

Quilting

Remove the freezer-paper templates. Prepare your quilt for quilting by adding the backing and batting, following the instructions on page xix. Quilt as shown in Diagram 7.

1. Quilt horizontally and vertically in the ditch (seam line) on each side of the sashing strip and around each petal.

2. Quilt ¼″ (64mm) on the inside of each petal.

3. Quilt the center circle as you choose.

4. Quilt the background with horizontal rows 1″ (2.5cm) apart.

Finishing the Quilt

Use the guidelines on page xix to finish the outside of the quilt with a narrow gold binding. To quilt the outside border:

1. Cut a plastic template 1″ × 8″ (2.5cm × 20.3cm). Beginning at the mitered corner, lay the template beside the mitered sewing line and mark the opposite side of the template lightly.

2. Continue moving toward the center of the border, drawing lines 1″ (2.5cm) apart (see Diagram 8). Begin at the opposite mitered seam and complete the lines you started from the other side. Fill in the entire side as shown.

3. Mark the other three sides in the same manner, and quilt along these lines.

4. Remove all the basting stitches.

Now relax under the peaceful beauty of your quilt.

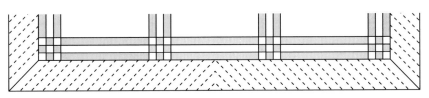

Diagram 8

Wild Goose Chase

63″ × 78″ (160cm × 198cm)

The quilt pictured uses several different ties. The geese are set in white. Wine and white nine patches make the corner squares for the white sashing. A narrow wine and a wider white border are finished with a narrow wine binding.

Wild Goose Chase

A variation of the Flying Geese pattern, WILD GOOSE CHASE is a traditional pieced block in which the geese fly toward a center square. It has been popular with the Amish, the Mennonites, and other groups since the early nineteenth century, and it is known by several names, including Old Fellows Block and Rambler.

This pattern can be pieced in all sizes with any number of fabrics and colors, and, although challenging, can be made by beginning quilters.

Choosing Fabrics

This pattern can take on many different looks depending on the placement of color. It can be made with dark geese surrounded by a light background or in the reverse. In the quilt pictured, the geese are made from many different colors. The large triangles in each block are made from one tie, as are the corner squares, but each block is different. The center squares are light yellows, creams, or beiges. White is used for the background triangles and for the sashing, while the nine-patch corner units are created from several ties of one color and contrast fabric. It is easier to make points on the geese if light-weight fabrics are used. Shiny ties make the geese stand out.

Block Construction

The finished size includes a 3″ (7.6cm) sashing and a 3″ (7.6cm) matching border, a 3″ (7.6cm) dark border, a 4½″ (11.4cm) light outer border, and a narrow binding. Blocks for all quilts are 12″ × 12″ (31cm × 31cm). Use the chart below to determine the number of blocks you will need.

	TWIN 63″ × 78″ (160cm × 198cm)	DOUBLE 78″ × 78″ (198cm × 198cm)	QUEEN 78″ × 93″ (198cm × 236cm)	KING 93″ × 93″ (236cm × 236cm)
Rows of blocks	3 × 4	4 × 4	4 × 5	5 × 5
Number of blocks	12	16	20	25
Number of nine-patch corner units	20	25	30	36

Fabric Requirements

Tie fabric makes up almost all of the block, with background fabric filling in the remainder.

Tie Fabric ～ *Number of templates needed*

	TWIN	DOUBLE	QUEEN	KING
Large triangles (template A)	48	64	80	100
Center squares (template B)	12	16	20	25
Corner squares (template C)	48	64	80	100
Goose triangles (template D)	96	128	160	200
Nine-patch squares —1½″ (3.8cm)	100	125	150	180

Background Fabric

	TWIN	DOUBLE	QUEEN	KING
Small triangles *(template E)*	288	384	480	600
Short border—*cut 2*	5″ × 54½″ (12.7cm × 138.4cm)	5″ × 69½″ (12.7cm × 176.5cm)	5″ × 69½″ (12.7cm × 176.5cm)	5″ × 84½″ (12.7cm × 214.6cm)
Long border—*cut 2*	5″ × 78½″ (12.7cm × 199.4cm)	5″ × 78½″ (12.7cm × 237.5cm)	5″ × 93½″ (12.7cm × 237.5cm)	5″ × 93½″ (12.7cm × 199.4cm)
Total fabric needed	2 yds (1.83m)	3 yds (2.74m)	3¼ yds (2.97m)	4¼ yds (3.89m)

Contrast Fabrics

	TWIN	DOUBLE	QUEEN	KING
Short border—*cut 2*	3½″ × 48½″ (8.9cm × 123.2cm)	3½″ × 63½″ (8.9cm × 161.3cm)	3½″ × 63½″ (8.9cm × 199.4cm)	3½″ × 78½″ (8.9cm × 199.4cmI)
Long border—*cut 2*	3½″ × 69½″ (8.9cm × 176.5cm)	3½″ × 69½″ (8.9cm × 176.5cm)	3½″ × 84½″ (8.9cm × 214.6cm)	3½″ × 84½″ (8.9cm × 214.6cm)
Nine-patch squares for corner units—1½″ × 1½″ (3.8cm)	80	100	120	144
Binding—2½″ (6.4cm) wide	310″ (7.87m)	335″ (8.51m)	380″ (9.65m)	395″ 10.33m
Total fabric needed	3 yds (2.74m)	3 yds (2.74m)	3¼ yds (2.97m)	3¼ yds (2.97m)

Other

	TWIN	DOUBLE	QUEEN	KING
Backing	5 yds (4.57m)	5 yds (4.57m)	5¾ yds (5.26m)	8½ yds (7.77m)

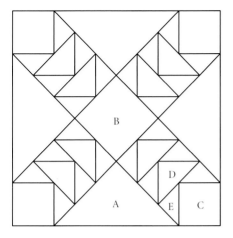

Diagram 1

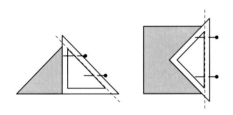

Diagram 2

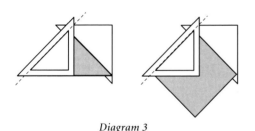

Diagram 3

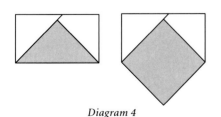

Diagram 4

Cutting

1. Using templates A through D (see Diagram 1) and following the charts above, cut out the required number of pieces from the tie fabric. Freezer-paper templates (page xvii) are recommended for this project. Press the templates for the geese (template D) to the right side of the ties so you can see the design you will be using. Cut, leaving ¼″ (64mm) from the edge of each template. Remove the freezer paper and press it to the back of each triangle. Cut all other template pieces as described on page xv. Stack or store pieces by block.

2. From the background fabric, first cut the long and short border pieces. Next, cut the required number of sashing strips. Using a rotary cutter, cut 2⅝″ × 2⅝″ (6cm × 6cm) squares that can be sectioned diagonally into the requisite number of small triangles (template E) for your quilt.

3. Cut the remaining border pieces and nine-patch squares from contrast fabric according to the charts above.

Making the Quilt Top

1. For each block, pin a small background triangle (template E) to one side of each corner square (template C) and to one side of each goose triangle (template D) as shown in Diagram 2. Chain sew each pinned seam using the freezer paper as a guide. Press the seams flat and cut apart. Trim the dark fabric seam allowance to a scant ¼″ (64mm) and press toward the light triangle (Diagram 2). Check the front to be sure the dark fabric doesn't show through. If it does, press to the dark triangle.

2. Follow the same process to add another background triangle to the opposite side of the goose triangle and to an adjoining side of the corner square, matching the points exactly (see Diagram 3). Snip all tails. The finished pieces should look like those in Diagram 4. Make eight unit A pieces and four unit B pieces.

3. Pin and sew two unit A pieces to form one segment (see Diagram 5); repeat to make three more segments. Join one unit B to the top of each segment. Press seams on the wrong side first, then on the right side.

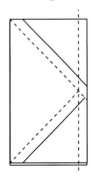

Diagram 5

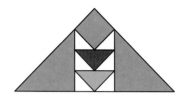

Diagram 6

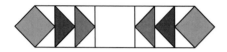

Diagram 7

Diagram 8

4. To assemble each block, sew one large triangle (template A) to each side of two goose segments to make a section like the one in Diagram 6; press seams toward the large triangles. Sew the other two goose segments to the opposite sides of a center square (template B) as in Diagram 7; press seams toward center. Join all three sections to form a block as shown in Diagram 8. Press carefully—do not stretch.

5. Square up the block on a 12½″ × 12½″ ruler, centering and aligning the lines on the ruler with the seams and corners of the block.

6. Lay out all finished blocks and arrange as desired. Label the backs of the blocks 1, 2, 3, and so on, in vertical rows (see Diagram 9).

7. Sew one piece of sashing to the bottom of blocks 1 through 3. Connect these squares to make one vertical row, adding block 4 at the bottom. Repeat for each row in the quilt. Press seams toward the sashing strips.

8. Make the required number of nine-patch corner units. Sew one corner unit to the bottom of each of three long sashing pieces; connect the three pieces to form a vertical strip. Make the required number of strips in the same way.

9. To connect the blocks, pin and sew a sashing strip to Row 1, matching all seams. Alternate rows of blocks with sashing strips until the quilt top is complete. Press seams toward sashing.

Making the Border

1. Make two short and two long sashing borders, alternating sashing strips and nine-patch squares to fit your quilt. Attach to the quilt and press.

2. Pin and sew first the short, then the long, border pieces (contrast fabric) to the sides of the quilt. Press seams outward. Add the wide border (background fabric) in the same way.

Quilting

Prepare your quilt for quilting by adding the backing and batting, following the instructions on page xii.

1. Quilt ¼″ (64mm) inside the seam line on all patches in each block (see Diagram 10). Quilt a triangle ½″ (1.3cm) inside each large triangle. Quilt each center square and corner square from corner to corner.

2. Quilt in the ditch in all squares of the nine-patch corner units. Quilt the sashing strips and border following the lines of the nine-patch.

3. Quilt the 3″ (6.4cm) border in 1″ (2.5cm) squares.

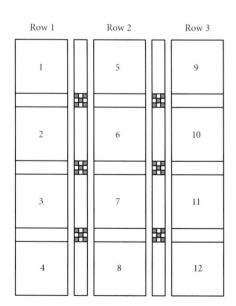

Diagram 9

Diagram 10

Finishing the Quilt

Finish the edge of the quilt following the guidelines on page xix. Quilt the wide outer border with straight lines spaced 1″ (2.5cm) apart. Make and sew on the binding following the instructions on page xix.

Variations

1. Ties may be used for every piece in the blocks.
2. The center squares, corner squares, and outer border would be pretty quilted with acorn or oak leaf patterns.

Years after making this quilt, I still love its beauty and the memories that go with it.

Ocean Waves

57″ × 81″ (145cm × 206cm)

A study in contrasts, half of the waves in this quilt are made from tie fabrics in blues, reds, greens, and golds. The other half is made up of white fabric, and the whole design is set off by navy blue center squares, background, borders, and binding.

Ocean Waves

OCEAN WAVES is one of the oldest and most popular of all the traditional pieced quilt designs, its origins going back to the Pennsylvania Amish and
Mennonites around 1890. The pattern always seems to show motion—white
or light triangles alternate with darker colors to mimic the whitecaps seen
on the crests of waves.

This is a very bright, vibrant design which can be interpreted in many
ways and looks lovely in any size quilt. One of the more complicated pieced
patterns, Ocean Waves is a block made up of four six-sided units of 24 triangles each. Although all of the units are the same, they are set together so
light and dark fabrics alternate.

Choosing Fabrics

I chose to use a silky navy blue fabric for the center of the blocks and the
wide border, with a white-on-white textured fabric with no shine for half of
the triangles to emulate waves. For the other half of the triangles, or waves,
I chose various hues of reds and blues with a few golds and greens mixed in.
All of the colored fabrics are lustrous, contrasting in texture with the matte
finish of the white pieces to give the feeling of the ocean's ebb and flow.

As a rough estimate of color division, plan to cut two-thirds of the tie
triangles from the blue family, one-sixth from the red family, and one-
twelfth each from the green and gold groups. In other words, for every eight
blue triangles you cut, you should have two red, one gold, and one green.
Since the pieces are small, light-weight ties work well.

Block Construction

The final size of each quilt includes a 10½″ (26.7cm) border and a narrow
binding. Each block in all quilts is 12″ × 12″ (30.1cm × 30.1cm). Use the
chart below to determine the number of blocks you will need.

	TWIN 57″ × 81″ 144.8cm × 205.7cm	DOUBLE 69″ × 81″ 175.2cm × 205.7cm	QUEEN 81″ × 93″ 205.7cm × 236.2cm	KING 93″ × 93″ 236.2cm × 236.2cm
Rows of blocks	3 × 5	4 × 5	5 × 6	6 × 6
Total number of blocks	15	20	30	36
Total number of pieced hexagons	60	80	120	144
Total number of wave triangles (*template A*)	1440	1920	2880	3456

Fabric Requirements

The waves in Ocean Waves use equal amounts of tie fabric and white contrast fabric. A background fabric of dark blue is used for the border, center squares, and triangles that fill in the blocks.

To estimate the number of ties you will need, see how many templates fit on one tie. Divide the total number of triangles you need by this number. A contrast fabric—white in the quilt photographed—is used for the tops of the waves.

Tie Fabric 〜 Number of templates needed

	TWIN	DOUBLE	QUEEN	KING
Wave triangles (template A)	720	960	1440	1728

Background Fabric

	TWIN	DOUBLE	QUEEN	KING
Center squares (template B)	23	32	50	61
Outside triangles (template C)	12	14	18	20
Corner triangles (template D)	4	4	4	4
Short outside border—cut 2	11″ × 36½″ (27.9cm × 92.7cm)	11″ × 48½″ (27.9cm × 123.2cm)	11″ × 60½″ (27.9cm × 153.7cm)	11″ × 72½″ (27.9cm × 184.2cm)
Long outside border—cut 2	11″ × 81½″ (27.9cm × 207cm)	11″ × 81½″ (27.9cm × 207cm)	11″ × 93½″ (27.9cm × 237.5cm)	11″ × 93½″ (27.9cm × 237.5cm)
Binding—2″ (5.1cm) wide	275″ (6.99cm)	310″ (7.87cm	360″ (9.14cm)	385″ (9.09cm)
Total fabric needed	3½ yds (3.2m)	3¾ yds (3.43m)	4½ yds (4.11m)	4¾ yds (4.34m)

Contrast Fabric

	TWIN	DOUBLE	QUEEN	KING
Wave triangles (template A)	720	960	1440	1728
Total fabric needed	1¾ yds (1.6m)	2 yds (1.83m)	3 yds (2.74m)	3¾ yds (3.43m)

Other

	TWIN	DOUBLE	QUEEN	KING
Backing (cotton fabric)	5 yds (4.57m)	5 yds (4.57m)	5½ yds (5.03m)	8¼ yds (7.54m)

Cutting

1. Using template A and following the charts above, cut out the required number of pieces from the tie fabric. Freezer-paper templates (page xv) are recommended for this project. Freezer-paper triangles can be made quickly by cutting the paper into strips 1½″ (3.8cm) wide. Cut these strips into 1½″ × 1½″ (3.8cm × 3.8cm) squares, then cut corner to corner using a rotary cutter.

2. The following table will help you decide how many triangles (template A) of each color you will need to cut for the tie part of the waves.

	TWIN	DOUBLE	QUEEN	KING
Blues, medium and dark	480	640	960	1,152
Reds	120	160	240	288
Greens	60	80	120	144
Golds	60	80	120	144

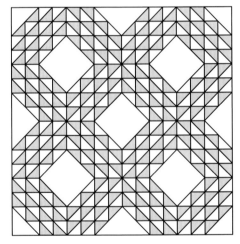

Diagram 1

3. Divide up the tie triangles for each hexagon. As stated earlier, for every eight blue triangles you cut, you should have two red, one gold, and one green. Use this rule for each hexagon in your quilt, following the charts above for total number needed. For a twin-size quilt, you will have 60 storage bags.

4. Diagram 1 shows a small version of the quilt to help you visualize where extra fabric pieces go. For the navy background fabric, cut the long border strips side by side, parallel to the selvage. Cut the short borders next, continuing down the selvage. Cut the binding and remaining pieces using the charts above and templates B, C, and D as guides.

5. Cut the required number of white triangles (template A) from the contrast fabric. Put 12 in each bag or stack of tie templates.

Making the Quilt Top

1. Lay out the 24 triangles (12 white and 12 tie fabric) in one bag or stack as in Diagram 2. Check for the best color placement. Have 20 or more extra color triangles on hand so you can switch them as necessary while you are pinning each group together. Following the diagram, label each tie triangle, 1, 2, 3, and so on.

2. Turn tie triangle 1 on top of a white triangle and pin at each end of the freezer paper (see Diagram 3). Continue pinning the remaining pieces and chain sew (see page xv) all pinned seams. Press flat, trim seams to a scant ¼″ (64mm), cut apart, and press seams toward the dark triangle. Check each square to be sure it is exactly 2″ (5.1cm). Lay the pieces out again, following Diagram 2.

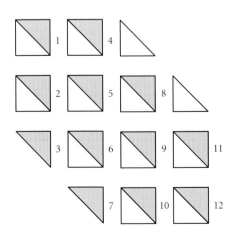

Diagram 2

⌒ Use a scrap saver or a 4″ x 4″ (10.2cm) transparent square ruler to check size. On a cutting mat, line up the 45-degree line with the seam line of the two triangles. Hold the ruler down tightly, and use a rotary cutter to trim two sides. Turn the square around and align the two edges you just trimmed on the 2″ (5.1cm) lines. With the 45-degree line again on the center seam, trim the other two sides.

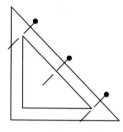

Diagram 3

3. Pin and chain sew the triangle-squares into rows. Pin square 1 to square 2, square 4 to square 5, square 6 to square 7, a white triangle to square 8, square 9 to square 10, and square 11 to square 12. Sew triangle 3 to the bottom of Row 1 and a white triangle to the top of Row 4. Press flat, and cut apart. Press the seams in Rows 1 and 3 toward the light triangles and the seams in Rows 2 and 4 toward the dark triangles—this will make it easier to join the rows into a hexagon.

4. Lay out the rows again as in Diagram 2, and carefully pin Row 1 to Row 2 and Row 3 to Row 4, matching seams perfectly. Sew. Pin and sew Rows 2 and 3 together. Press the seams toward Rows 2 and 4. Repeat until you have the requisite number of hexagons for your quilt.

5. Lay out the entire quilt following Diagram 4 for a double quilt. Adapt the diagram as necessary for different size quilts. When blocks are arranged as you want them, label each of the four hexagons in the first block A, B, C, and D (see Diagram 5) and store in a bag labeled block 1. Repeat for all other blocks.

6. Mark the center of each side of the center square (see Diagram 6). Pin a hexagon to one side of the center square at the ¼″ (64mm) seam allowance, matching the center point of the dark triangle to the marked point on the side. Sew from seam allowance to seam allowance. Working clockwise, pin and sew on the rest of the hexagons.

Diagram 4

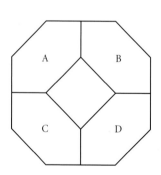

Diagram 5

Diagram 6

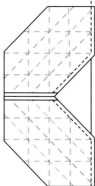

Diagram 7

Row 1

Row 2

Row 3

Row 4

Row 5

Diagram 8

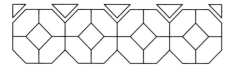

Diagram 9

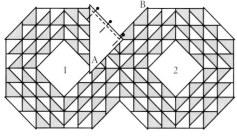

Diagram 10

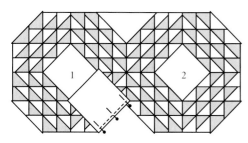

Diagram 11

7. Fold the block in half diagonally (see Diagram 7), pin and sew the seam at each end that joins two hexagons, matching the triangle points carefully. Now fold in half the other way, pin, and sew the last two seams of the hexagon. Press the seams from the wrong side, then from the right side. Repeat until all blocks are made.

8. Arrange the pieced octagons in horizontal rows according to your quilt size, as in Diagram 8. Pin octagon 1 to octagon 2 and sew from seam allowance to seam allowance. Continue until all horizontal rows have been joined. Press all seams in each row.

9. For Row 1, pin and sew on the two navy corner triangles (template D) as in Diagram 9. For each outside navy triangle (template C), pin and sew one side of the triangle between two octagons (see Diagram 10), sewing from the center out. Backstitch at the beginning. Following the diagram, bring point A to point B, pin this side of the triangle to the second octagon, and sew as described. Repeat the process for the corner and outside triangles at the bottom of Row 5.

10. Using the same technique, sew two sides of the center squares (template B) between each of the four octagons at the bottom of Row 1, backstitching as described. (See Diagram 11.) Repeat for squares at the bottom of Rows 2 through 4. Press every seam.

11. Connect the rows and press. Pin and sew in the outside triangles on both sides of the quilt. Press.

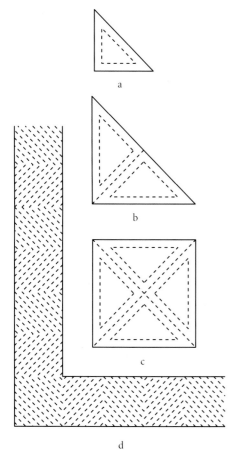

a

b

c

d

Diagram 12

Making the Border

1. Sew on the top and bottom borders, pinning the center, ends, and middle before you sew. Press the seams toward the border.
2. Follow the same procedure for the side borders.

Quilting

Prepare your quilt for quilting by adding the backing and batting, following the instructions on page xix. Quilt as in Diagram 12.

1. Quilt ¼″ (64mm) inside each small triangle. This gives a lot of dimension.
2. Quilt the center squares and outside and corner triangles.
3. Quilt the border in pointed waves spaced 1½″ (3.8cm) apart.

Finishing the Quilt

Finish the edge of the quilt following the guidelines on page xix. Quilt the border as desired. Make and sew on the binding following the instructions on page xix.

Variations

1. Instead of the 10½″ (26.7cm) border, you may substitute a 3″ (7.6cm) inner border and a 7½″ (19.1cm) outer border.
2. The borders can be quilted in sea patterns, such as starfish, clam shells, or a variety of seashells, to enhance the ocean motif.
3. An attractive alternative to binding this quilt is to use a Prairie Point border. Cut 2½″ (6.4cm) squares, using all the colors in the waves including white. You will need 140 squares for a twin quilt, 156 for a double, 176 for a queen, and 188 for a king. Press each square in half diagonally, right side out. Fold in half again to make the prairie point.

To attach the prairie points, trim the batting even with the edge of the quilt top, but do not trim the backing. Arrange the prairie points along the edge of the quilt top, placing the cut edge of each even with the raw edge of the quilt top. The point is toward the center of the quilt (see Diagram 13). Fit the prairie points inside each other, overlapping by a generous ¼″ (64mm). For a twin quilt, you will need 29 points on each short side and 41 on each long side; for a double, 35 on each short side and 41 on each long side; for a queen, 41 on each short side and 47 on each long side; and for a king, 47 on each side.

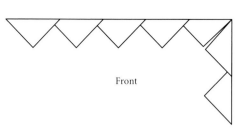

Front

Diagram 13

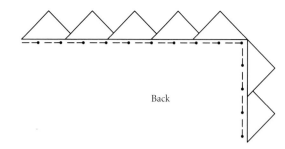

Back

Diagram 14

Pin each point in place and stitch ¼″ (64mm) from the edge of the quilt top. Sew through the points and the quilt top only. Complete all four sides and press the points outward, pressing the seam toward the wide border.

Trim backing ½″ (1.3cm) larger than the top. Working from the back, fold under the raw edge of the backing and pin in place, covering the raw edge of the prairie points (see Diagram 14). Blindstitch to the back of the prairie points. Remove all basting threads.

Seven Sisters

58″ × 85″ (147cm × 216cm)

Seven Sisters is an enchanting pattern in which six tie diamonds in various blues make up the stars (sisters), surrounded by white diamonds and trapezoids to form a hexagon-shaped block. These are set together with navy triangles. A white and navy border frames the quilt, which is finished with a narrow navy binding.

Seven Sisters

Since the nineteenth century, quilters have loved this design for its beauty and for its romantic associations. In Greek mythology, Atlas and Plelone had seven daughters who were pursued by Orion, an amorous hunter. To protect the sisters, Zeus changed them into stars and placed them in the heavens. This star cluster is known as Pleiades, and its rising is a sign of clear sailing.

SEVEN SISTERS is a difficult pattern to sew by machine but is easy when hand sewn, using English paper piecing (see page xv). It looks pretty in any size. The width is easily increased by adding one or more blocks to each row. To keep the pattern consistent, length must be added or taken away two rows at a time.

Choosing Fabrics

The quilt shown uses blue tie fabrics or tie fabrics with some blue in them for the stars. Because the pieces are small, light-weight, shimmery fabrics are perfect. You will need a white or cream fabric for the background diamonds and trapezoids that connect the sisters and a contrast fabric for the triangles that connect the blocks

Block Construction

As you look at the blocks in the quilt, notice that each is comprised of seven stars. These are constructed first, and are then joined to the twelve white diamonds. They are then surrounded by more diamonds and trapezoids. Block size for all quilt sizes is 11″ × 12½″ (28cm × 31.8cm). The final size includes a mitered 1″ (2.5cm) white border and a 3″ (7.6cm) contrast border and a narrow binding. Use the chart below to determine the number of blocks you will need.

	TWIN 58″ × 85″ 147.3cm × 215.9cm	DOUBLE 70½″ × 85″ 179.1cm × 215.9cm	QUEEN 83″ × 107″ 210.8cm × 271.8cm	KING 95½″ × 107″ 242.6cm × 271.8cm
Rows of blocks (see Diagram 1)	4 × 7	5 × 7	6 × 9	7 × 9
Number of whole blocks	25	32	50	59
Number of half blocks	6	6	8	8
Number of stars	193	242	374	437

Fabric Requirements

SEVEN SISTERS uses ties for all the stars against a white background fabric that is also used for the narrow inner border. A navy contrast fabric sets the blocks together and is used for the wider outside border and binding.

Tie Fabric ~ *Number of templates needed*

	TWIN	DOUBLE	QUEEN	KING
Diamonds (template A)	1,182	1,476	2,276	2,654

Background Fabric

	TWIN	DOUBLE	QUEEN	KING
Diamonds *(template A)*	498	624	964	1,126
Trapezoids *(template B)*	162	204	316	370
Half diamonds *(half template A)*	12	12	16	16
Half trapezoids *(half template B)*	12	12	16	16
Short mitered border—*cut 2*	1½″ × 62″ (8cm × 157.5cm)	1½″ × 74½″ (3.8cm × 189.2cm)	1½″ × 87″ (3.8cm × 221cm)	1½″ × 99½″ (3.8cm × 252.7cm)
Long mitered border—*cut 2*	1½″ × 89″ (3.8cm × 226.1cm)	1½″ × 89″ (3.8cm × 226.1cm)	1½″ × 111″ (3.8cm × 282cm)	1½″ × 111″ (3.8cm × 282cm)
Total fabric needed	2¾ yds (2.51m)	3½ yds (3.2m)	3½ yds (3.2m)	4 yds (3.66m)

Contrast Fabric

	TWIN	DOUBLE	QUEEN	KING
Connecting triangles *(template C)*	48	62	98	116
Half connecting triangles *(half template C)*	16	16	20	20
Short mitered border—*cut 2*	3½ × 62″ (8.9cm × 157.5cm)	3½″ × 74½″ (8.9cm × 189.2cm)	3½″ × 87″ (8.9cm × 221cm)	3½″ × 99½″ (8.9cm × 252.7cm)
Long mitered border—*cut 2*	3½″ × 89″ (8.9cm × 226.1cm)	3½″ × 89″ (8.9cm × 226.1cm)	3½″ × 111″ (8.9cm × 282cm)	3½″ × 111″ (8.9cm × 282cm)
Binding—2″ (5.1cm) wide	300″ (7.62cm)	330″ (8.38cm)	390″ (9.91cm)	420″ (10.67cm)
Total fabric needed	3½ yds (3.2m)	3½ yds (3.2m)	4 yds (3.66m)	4¾ yds (4.34m)

Other

	TWIN	DOUBLE	QUEEN	KING
Backing	5 yds 4.57m	5¼ yds 4.8m	6¼ yds 5.72m	9½ yds 8.69m

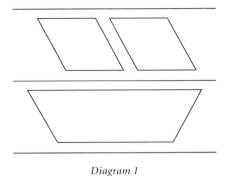

Diagram 1

Cutting

1. Using template A and following the charts above, cut out the required number of pieces from the tie fabric. Freezer-paper templates (page xv) are recommended for this project. Lay out 42 diamonds on one tie for one block, leaving ¼″ (64mm) for seam allowance. Store or stack template pieces by block.

2. First cut the long and short borders from the background fabric, then cut 1½″ (3.8cm) strips and press half templates A and B onto them (see Diagram 1). Cut.

3. Divide the total length of the binding by three, then cut three strips this length parallel to the selvage of the contrast fabric. Cut the two long borders parallel to the binding strips, then the short borders next to the long ones. Press templates and half templates C on remaining material as needed.

Making the Quilt Top

1. The English paper piecing method (page xv) is good for this project because the pieces are so small. Follow Diagram 2 to prepare the diamonds for this procedure. Fold side 1 over the paper and baste. Clip the point between sides 1 and 2 to ⅛″ (13mm) and fold upward toward the paper. Fold side 2 over the paper and baste. Repeat with sides 3 and 4. Baste three sides of each white trapezoid (see Diagram 3). Baste two sides of the six white diamonds (see Diagram 4).

2. Pin two diamonds together, right sides facing, and whip stitch one side together as shown in Diagram 5. Open and finger press. Add a third diamond and whip stitch in place (see Diagram 6). Make another set of

⁓ When basting the diamonds, leave a tail at the top of each diamond as you baste. When the diamonds are sewn into a star, these tails will be the center. This technique also creates less bulk in the star and stops a hole from occurring in the center of the star.

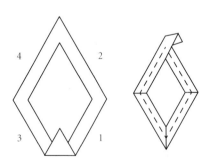

Diagram 2

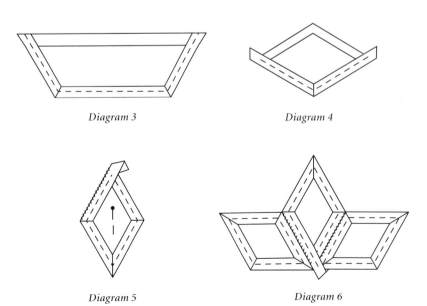

Diagram 3   *Diagram 4*

Diagram 5   *Diagram 6*

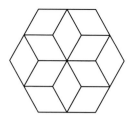

Diagram 7

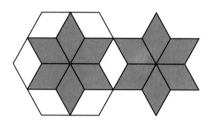

Diagram 8

three diamonds. Pin and sew the two sets of diamonds together, forming a star (see Diagram 7). Make sure the centers match perfectly. Repeat for all the stars in your quilt.

3. Whip stitch six white diamonds (template A) around one star (Diagram 8 shows a completed piece). Add stars around the outsides of the completed hexagon, adding remaining white diamonds as needed. Complete all blocks in this manner.

4. When all stars are sewn together, whip stitch the six basted trapezoids and the diamonds around the outside to form a larger hexagon. You will have raw edges around the outside.

5. Lay out the hexagons to form your desired pattern. Add the triangles as needed to fill in. Label each row and each block in the row: Row 1, Block A; Row 1, Block B; and so on. Store each row separately.

6. Sew the quilt together by rows (see Diagram 9): Attach half triangle a to Block A; half triangle b to Block A; triangle 2 to Block A; triangles 1 and 4 to Block B; triangles 3 and 6 to Block C; triangle 5 to Block D; half triangle c and triangle d to Block D. Sew these pieces together to form Row 1.

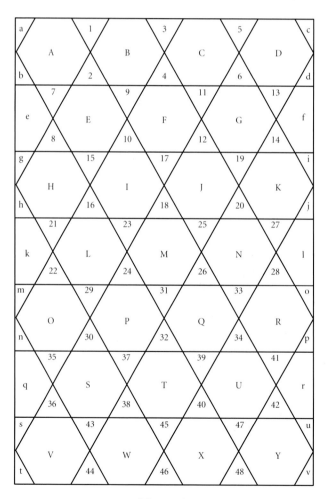

Diagram 9

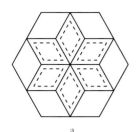

a

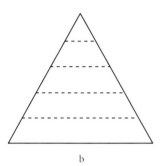

b

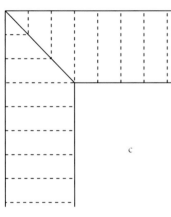

c

Diagram 10

7. Using Diagram 9 as a guide, repeat this process for all rows in the quilt. Press and lay out.

8. Pin and sew all the rows together, matching all seams exactly.

Making the Border

Sew the narrow white border to the wider navy border for all fours sides of the quilt and treat them as a single border as you sew them on. Sew on the two short borders, then the long borders. Press.

Quilting

Prepare your quilt for quilting by adding the backing and batting, following the instructions on page xix. Quilt as in Diagram 10.

1. Quilt ¼″ (64mm) from the seam lines on all diamonds and trapezoids.

2. Quilt straight lines 1″ (2.6cm) apart across the triangles.

3. Quilt the border with straight lines 1″ (2.6cm) apart and perpendicular to the outside edge of the quilt.

Finishing the Quilt

Finish the edge of the quilt following the guidelines on page xix. Make and sew on the binding following the instructions on page xix.

Variations

Each sister in a block can be made from a different color fabric, with all blocks alike. Choose pastels if you want a summery look.

Spools

72″ × 85″ (183cm × 216cm)

Contrasting tie fabrics are used for the spools in this quilt: blues for both ends and various colors for the middle. The pieced border employs pieces from all the ties. The background, outside border, and narrow binding are cream, while a dark burgundy is used for the lattice and narrow border.

Spools

ontrary to popular belief, this pattern was taken from the old-fashioned spool bed, or Jenny Lind, and not from spools of thread. Quilts with this design have been seen in varying forms as far back as the 1860s and were popular as frontier scrap quilts with American pioneer families. Some of the older quilts have blocks as small as 3″ (76cm). A 60″ × 84″ (203cm × 213.5cm) quilt would have 580 of these tiny blocks. This gave thrifty women a chance to use even their smallest scraps in a very beautiful way.

Achievable by beginners and a favorite with intermediate-level quilters, the pattern provides an opportunity to use many different tie fabrics. It can be made with or without sashing with very different effects.

Choosing Fabrics

I prefer to use shades of one color for all the spools, with various colors as the "thread," but you can make the spools many different colors and duplicate individual designs throughout the quilt. In using the same color of all the spool ends, make sure you have enough ties to cut two pieces for each spool. To pick out the thread fabrics, lay the spool color on other ties until you get a color combination you like. A neutral color, such as the cream-colored fabric used here, makes a good choice for the background pieces. Since the pieces are fairly large, any weight of fabric works well.

I have seen this pattern put together in so many ways. I know you will enjoy experimenting with the colors in your tie collection. Spools can be attached one to the other through the entire quilt, or fours spools can be put together in one larger square and set together with rows of narrow sashing, as in the quilt photographed.

Block Construction

Four spools are joined in a larger square and set together with rows of narrow sashing. I recommend making each spool section 6″ × 6″ (15.2cm), with four sections making a 12″ (30.5cm) square.

The finished size includes 1″ (2.5cm) sashing and a 1″ (2.5cm) matching border, a 2″ (5.1cm) cream border, a 1″ (2.5cm) pieced border, and a narrow cream binding. Each block in the table is 12″ × 12″ (30.5cm). Use the chart below to determine the number of blocks you will need.

	TWIN 59″ × 85″ (150cm × 216cm)	DOUBLE 72″ × 85″ (183cm × 216cm)	QUEEN 85″ × 98″ (216cm × 249cm)	KING 98″ × 98″ (216cm × 249cm)
Rows of blocks	4 × 6	5 × 6	6 × 7	7 × 7
Number of blocks	24	30	42	49
Total number of spools	96	120	168	196

Fabric Requirements

SPOOLS uses ties for the two spool ends, the center section, and the pieced border. A soft, silky burgundy is used for the sashing and border. The background and outer border are made of a cream-on-cream textured fabric.

It is difficult to calculate the number of ties needed for this quilt. If you are using a striped tie and want the same design on each spool end, you will probably be able to cut three or four pieces from the same tie. If you have a tie with an overall design (or a solid), it can probably give you eight or ten pieces.

Template A is used for the background pieces as well as for the spool ends. The background pieces may be cut from tie fabric if you prefer. Whatever fabric you use, you will need the same total yardage of background fabric to avoid having seams in your border pieces.

Tie Fabric ⁓ Number of templates needed

	TWIN	DOUBLE	QUEEN	KING
Spool ends (template A)	192	240	336	392
Border pieces, cut 1″ × 1½″ (2.5cm × 3.8cm)	576	628	732	784
Border corner pieces, cut 1½″ × 1½″ (3.8cm × 3.8cm)	4	4	4	4

Background Fabric

	TWIN	DOUBLE	QUEEN	KING
Side pieces (template A)	192	240	336	392
Short mitered border—cut 2	2½″ × 61″ (6.4cm × 154.9cm)	2½″ × 74″ (6.4cm × 188cm)	2½″ × 87″ (6.4cm × 220.9cm)	2½″ × 100″ (6.4cm × 254cm)
Long mitered border—cut 2	2½″ × 87″ (6.4cm × 220.9cm)	2½″ × 87″ (6.4cm × 220.9cm)	2½″ × 100″ (6.4cm × 254cm)	2½″ × 100″ (6.4cm × 254cm)
Binding 2½″ (6.4cm) wide	305″ (7.75m)	330″ (8.38m)	382″ (9.7m)	410″ (10.41m)
Total fabric needed	3 yds (2.74m)	3½ yds (3.2m)	4½ yds (4.11m)	5 yds (4.57m)

Contrast Fabric

	TWIN	DOUBLE	QUEEN	KING
Short sashing strips, cut 1½″ × 12½″ (3.8cm × 31.8cm)	20	25	36	42
Long sashing strips cut size	3 1½″ × 77½″ (3.8cm × 196.9cm)	4 1½″ × 77½″ (3.8cm × 196.9cm)	5 1½″ × 90½″ (3.8cm × 229.9cm)	6 1½″ × 90½″ (3.8cm × 229.9cm)
Short matching border—cut 2	1½″ × 51½″ (3.8cm × 130.8)	1½″ × 64½″ (3.8cm × 163.8cm)	1½″ × 77½″ (3.8cm × 196.9cm)	1½″ × 90½″ (3.8cm × 229.9cm)
Long matching border—cut 2	1½″ × 79½″ (3.8cm × 201.9cm)	1½″ × 79½″ (3.8cm × 201.9cm)	1½″ × 92½″ (3.8cm × 234.9cm)	1½″ × 92½″ (3.8cm × 234.9cm)
Total fabric needed	2½ yds (2.29m)	2½ yds (2.29m)	3 yds (2.74m)	3 yds (2.74m)

Other

	TWIN	DOUBLE	QUEEN	KING
Backing (cotton fabric)	5¼ yds (4.8m)	5¼ yds (4.8m)	6 yds (5.49m)	9 yds (8.23m)

⌣ Be sure to consider the design of each tie as you lay out your template. Striped fabric adds a lot of interest to the spool design but requires careful planning before cutting. Stripes should run straight across a template or on a diagonal. When using a striped tie for spool ends, ensure that the stripe looks the same on both ends.

Cutting

1. Using templates A and B and the charts above, cut and press freezer-paper templates (page xv) for the required pieces of tie fabric. Remember to leave ¼″ (64mm) around all templates for seam allowances.

2. Cut 2½″ (6.4cm) binding strips the full length of the background fabric, then cut the long and short borders. If you are using this fabric for the side pieces, cut the remaining fabric into 2″ (5.1cm) strips and cut the required number of templates from these strips.

3. Enough contrast fabric is allowed for the long sashing and long border pieces to be without seams, as long as they are cut before the shorter pieces.

Making the Quilt Top

1. Lay out all spool ends and thread pieces on a white or light sheet and match the colors and patterns as desired (do not worry about arranging the blocks yet). Pin the spool ends (template A) to their corresponding centers (template B) at the seam allowance as in Diagram 1, matching the template corners and making sure all fabric designs face the right direction.

2. Chain sew by machine one end piece to the center piece from pin to pin, backstitching two or three stitches on each end. Attach the other end piece in the same way and press seams away from the center. Pin two side pieces in place on each side of the spool (see Diagram 2). Sew both seams from pin to pin; press seams away from center.

3. To sew the four corner seams, fold the spool center piece in half diagonally. The ends will automatically fall in the correct direction, allowing you to pin and sew the two short seams from the center to the outside. Press seams open. Refold the square the opposite direction and sew the other two seams in the same way (see Diagram 3). Press. If needed, trim to a 6½″ (16.5cm) square.

4. When all spools are completed, lay them out as desired, alternating the direction of each spool (see Diagram 4). Label the spools by block (1A, 1B, 1C, and so on) as shown.

5. Pin and sew spool 1A to spool 1B and spool 1C to spool 1D. Press. Pin the two pieces together, matching the point where the four spools meet, and sew. Press. Repeat for each block.

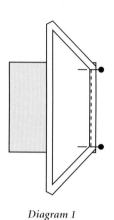

Diagram 1

~ Place a small X at the bottom of each spool so you will know which way to turn it when assembling the block.

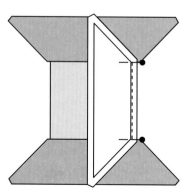

Diagram 2

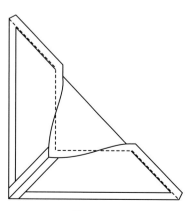

Diagram 3

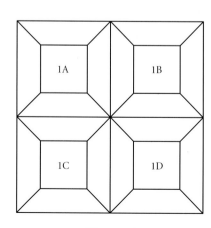

1A	1B
1C	1D

Diagram 4

Diagram 5

6. Lay out all quilt blocks with short sashing strips in place (see Diagram 5). Pin and sew a short sashing strip to the bottom of blocks 1, 2, and so on in Row 1. Repeat for the remaining rows. Connect the sashing at the bottom of block 1 to the top of block 2, and continue to connect the rest of the blocks in each row in the same way. Press seams toward the sashing.

7. Pin and sew a long sashing strip to Rows 1, 2, 3, and so on. Connect all rows. Press.

Making the Borders

1. Sew the short contrast borders to the top and bottom of the quilt top. Sew the long contrast borders to the sides of the quilt top.

2. Pin and sew the two short cream borders from seam allowance to seam allowance. Do the same with the two long cream borders. Press. Miter the corners (page xvi) and press again.

3. For the pieced border, arrange all the tie pieces for one side of the quilt, intermixing the colors. Chain sew them together in pairs and press. Join the pairs into fours and press again. Continue connecting pieces until you have a complete strip. Repeat for the other three quilt sides. Attach a 1½″ × 1½″ (3.8cm) square to each end of the long border strips and press. Pin and sew the two short borders, then the two long borders, to the quilt. Press seams toward the cream border.

Quilting

Prepare your quilt for quilting by adding the backing and batting, following the instructions on page xix. The quilting plan for this project is fairly simple (see Diagram 6).

1. Quilt in the ditch (seam line) around each block next to the sashing.

2. Quilt five evenly spaced lines across the thread and three evenly spaced lines across the spool ends.

3. Quilt ¼″ (64mm) inside the edge of the side pieces of each spool.

4. Quilt in the ditch on the outside of the sashing border and ¼″ (64mm) from the edge around the cream border, or as desired.

5. Quilt in the ditch next to the pieced border.

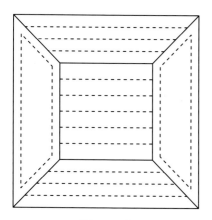

Diagram 6

Finishing the Quilt

Finish the edge of the quilt following the guidelines on page xix. Make and sew on the cream binding following the instructions on page xix.

This delightful quilt will look great not only on a bed, but on a wall or over a staircase banister as well.

Nosegay

37″ × 37″ (94cm × 94cm)

The small quilt or wall hanging shown is made exactly as a larger quilt would be. It shows how a few bouquets can be used as a very pretty accent. The soft green contrast block is perfect with the yellows, pinks, and aqua-blues of the flowers. A cream background fills in around the flowers.

Nosegay

*T*his delightful pattern of spring flowers is a version of the traditional Eight-Pointed Star pattern. It was inspired by the small bouquets of fresh mixed flowers that French street vendors wrapped in green tissue paper and sold to men as gifts for their girlfriends. Other names for this design include Bride's Bouquet, French Nosegay, and Cornucopia.

Because of the many set-in seams, NOSEGAY is fairly complex to make. The pattern looks lovely when set on point.

Choosing Fabrics

This quilt is gorgeous when made in the traditional way with green ties used for the paper wrapper. There are many ways to approach the flowers, such as using one tie for all three flowers in a block or making each flower from a different tie to give the impression of a mixed bouquet. Squares representing the flower centers may be made from one tie or two or three in similar colors. If you use a stripe, be sure to turn the stripes in the same direction and cut in the same place on the stripe whenever possible. Do not use a jacquard fabric for the background. The flower centers are easy to set in if made from lightweight ties. The larger pieces should also be made from light- to medium-weight fabrics. I prefer to use a light background color to make the flowers really stand out.

Block Construction

The finished size of this quilt includes a 4″ (10.2cm) border and a narrow binding. The block size for all quilts is 12″ × 12″ (30.5cm), with a diagonal width of 17″ (43.2cm). The small quilt pictured has a 1½″ (3.8cm) border made of strips of tie fabric 1″ (2.5cm) wide. Use the chart below to determine how many blocks you will need.

	TWIN 59″ × 76″ (149.9cm × 193cm)	DOUBLE 76″ × 93″ (193cm × 236.2cm)	QUEEN 93″ × 93″ (236.2cm × 236.2cm)	KING 110″ × 110″ (279.4cm × 279.4cm)
Rows of blocks	3 × 4	4 × 5	5 × 5	6 × 6
Number of nosegay blocks	12	20	25	36
Number of background blocks	6	12	16	25

Fabric Requirements

You will need tie fabric, background fabric, and a border fabric for this project. The border fabric should complement the tie fabrics in your flowers. Extra fabric has been added to the border measurements to allow for mitered corners.

Tie Fabric ~ *Number of template pieces needed*

	TWIN	DOUBLE	QUEEN	KING
Flower holders *(template A)*	12	20	25	36
Flower petals *(template B)*	72	120	150	216
Flower centers *(template D)*	60	100	125	180

Background Fabric

	TWIN	DOUBLE	QUEEN	KING
Templates C and CR *(each)*	12	20	25	36
Corners *(templates E and ER)*	36	60	75	108
Triangles *(template F)*	48	80	100	144
Short mitered border—*cut 2*	4½″ × 63″ (11.4cm ×160cm)	4½″ × 80″ (11.4cm × 203.2cm)	4½″ × 97″ (11.4cm ×246.4cm)	4½″ × 114″ (11.4cm ×289.6cm)
Long mitered border —*cut 2*	4½″ × 80″ (11.4cm × 203.2cm)	4½″ × 97″ (11.4cm × 246.4cm)	4½″ × 97″ (11.4cm × 246.4cm)	4½″ × 114″ (11.4cm × 289.6cm)
Binding 2″ (5.1cm wide)	285″ (7.24m)	355″ (9.01m)	390″ (9.9m)	455″ (11.56m)
Total fabric needed	2½ yds (2.29m)	3 yds (2.74m)	4 yds (3.66m)	5 yds (4.57m)

Contrast Fabric

	TWIN	DOUBLE	QUEEN	KING
Background squares	6	12	16	25
Outside triangles	10	14	16	20
Corner triangles	4	4	4	4
Total fabric needed	2½ yds (2.29m)	2¾ yds (2.51m)	3 yds (2.74m)	3½ yards (3.2m)

Other

	TWIN	DOUBLE	QUEEN	KING
Backing	4¾ yds (4.34m)	5¾ yds (5.26m)	8½ yds (7.77m)	9¾ yds (8.92m)

Cutting

1. Using templates A, B, and D and following the charts above, cut out the required number of pieces from the tie fabric. Freezer-paper templates (page xv) are recommended for this project. Store or stack template pieces by block.

2. Cut the binding strips parallel to the selvage on the background fabric. Next cut the border pieces.

3. Using templates C, CR, E, ER, and F, along with the charts above, cut the remaining template pieces from the background fabric. Separate pieces by block and place them with corresponding tie-fabric templates. Keep reverse pieces separate from other pieces in a block.

4. Cut the border pieces parallel to the selvage on the contrast fabric. Cut the 12½″ (31.8cm) squares and the 13″ (33cm) squares to make the outside triangles. Cut the 9½″ (24.1cm) squares to make the corner triangles.

Making the Quilt Top

1. Lay out the pieces one block at a time (see Diagram 1). Each block will be made into five separate units before being joined (see Diagram 2). When pinning the sections together, insert a pin at each end of the freezer paper first, then in other places as needed. Always press before sewing a second piece to a unit. You may wish to use the English paper piecing method (see page xv).

2. For Unit 1, pin and sew three sets of flower petals (template B) as in Diagram 3.

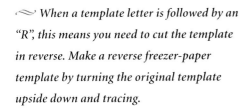 *When a template letter is followed by an "R", this means you need to cut the template in reverse. Make a reverse freezer-paper template by turning the original template upside down and tracing.*

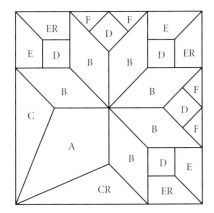

Diagram 1

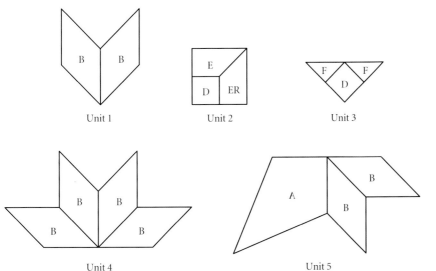

Unit 1   Unit 2   Unit 3

Unit 4   Unit 5

Diagram 2

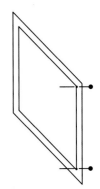

Diagram 3

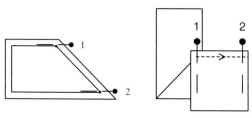

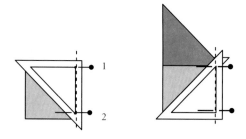

Diagram 4

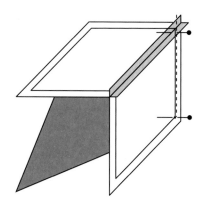

Diagram 5

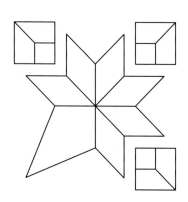

Diagram 6

Diagram 7

3. For Unit 2, pin and sew three sets of templates E and ER together. Then pin and sew from the first pin off the opposite edge (see Diagram 4). Pin and sew the other side in the same way.

4. For Unit 3, pin two sets of templates D and F together (see Diagram 5). Then pin and sew the second triangle from edge to edge.

5. Sew two Unit 1 sections together to form Unit 4 and sew the remaining Unit 1 section to the flower holder (template A) from one edge to the second pin to make Unit 5 (see Diagram 6).

6. Pin and sew two Unit 2 segments to Unit 4 and one Unit 2 segment to Unit 5 as in Diagram 7. Pin and sew the two large segments together as in Diagram 8, matching the center points exactly. Pin and sew the two Unit 3 segments in place, beginning at the center and sewing to the edge in both directions (see Diagram 9). To complete the block, sew in the two template C pieces from the center point to the edge in both directions.

7. Give the block a final pressing and square up if necessary. Repeat for all blocks in the quilt.

8. Lay out the pieced blocks on point with the background blocks, outside triangles, and corner triangles (see Diagram 10). Number the pieced blocks, and label the background blocks A, the outside triangles B, and the corner triangles C.

9. Connect the blocks in each diagonal row and add the two remaining corner triangles.

10. Connect the diagonal rows into a quilt top and give it a final press.

Making the Border

Sew on the short, then the long, borders and press seams outward. Miter the corners (page xvi).

Quilting

Prepare your quilt for quilting by adding the backing and batting, following the instructions on page xix.

1. Quilt in the ditch (seam line) around each block and ¼″ (64mm) from the edge of the flower petals and all background pieces (see Diagram 11).

2. Quilt radiating lines from the point to the top edge of the flower holder and from the flower to the outside edge of the flower centers.

3. In the plain blocks, quilt diagonal lines 1″ (2.5cm) apart in both directions to form diagonal squares, or use a design of your choice.

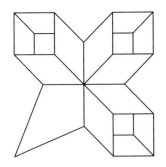

Diagram 8

Finishing the Quilt

Finish the edge of the quilt following the guidelines on page xix. Quilt the border as desired. Make and sew on the binding following the instructions on page xix.

Feel a refreshing lift every time you look at this spring-like work of art.

Diagram 9

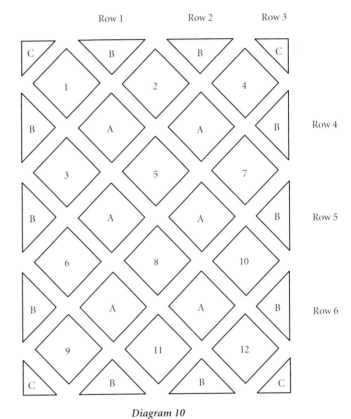

Diagram 10

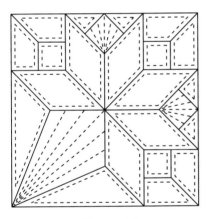

Diagram 11

Flying Swallows

32½″ × 45″ (83cm × 114cm)

Tie factory cuttings in dark lavender patterns have been used for the swallows, sashing, borders, and binding of this quilt. All other pieces are of cream polished cotton, providing sharp edges and bright contrast.

Flying Swallows

*F*LYING SWALLOWS is a traditional pattern dating from the 1800s, and the original was done in the same 12″ (30.5cm) square used here. Also known as Circling Swallows and Falling Stars, this beautiful design conveys a sense of movement and energy. Its delicate pattern is enchanting when made as a baby quilt, although it is equally charming as a bed-size quilt. Intermediate or advanced quilting skills are required for this pattern.

Choosing Fabrics

The fabrics and colors you choose for this project will depend on the small size of the diamonds that make up the swallows and on the size of your quilt. Opt for lightweight ties, as heavier fabrics do not work well with the small patches and many seams in this pattern. Look for solid colors or very small designs with no more than two colors. Fabrics with large designs of lots of colors tend to look blurry when cut into small pieces. This pattern is lovely using shades of one color on a white or cream background.

Block Construction

The finished size includes ½″ (1.3cm) sashing, a 1″ (2.5cm) sawtooth border, a 2½″ (6.4cm) to 4½″ (11.4cm) outer border, and a narrow binding. The block size for all quilts is 12″ × 12″ (30.5cm × 30.5cm). Use the chart below to determine how many blocks you will need.

	BABY 32½″ × 45″ (82.6cm × 114.3cm)	TWIN 58½″ × 83½″ (148.6cm × 212.1cm)	DOUBLE 84½″ × 84½″ (214.7cm × 214.7cm)	QUEEN 85½″ × 98″ (217.2cm × 249cm)	KING 99″ × 99″ (251.5cm × 251.5cm)
Row of blocks	2 × 3	4 × 6	6 × 6	6 × 7	7 × 7
Number of blocks	6	24	36	42	49
Total number of swallows	48	192	288	336	392
Outer border width	2½″ (6.4cm)	3″ (7.6cm)	3½″ (8.9cm)	4″ (10.2cm)	4½″ (11.4cm)

Fabric Requirements

Much of this quilt is made from background fabric, with the tie fabric reserved for the swallows and accents in the sashing, border, and binding. A polished cotton gives a shiny frame to the very soft tie fabric.

Since only 24 small diamonds are needed for the swallows in each block, you can use one tie for each block and easily have leftover fabric for the sawtooth border. This pattern is easier to piece and quilt if you stabilize the tie fabric with sheer fusible interfacing (page xvi).

Tie Fabric ~ Number of templates needed

	BABY	TWIN	DOUBLE	QUEEN	KING
Swallow diamonds (template A)	144	576	864	1,008	1,176
Border triangles (template E)	70	140	168	182	196

Background Fabric

	BABY	TWIN	DOUBLE	QUEEN	KING
Triangles (template B)	192	768	1,152	1,344	1,568
Corner squares (template C)	24	96	144	168	196
Large triangles (template D)	24	96	144	168	196
Border triangles (template E)	66	136	164	178	192
Short mitered border—cut 2	3″ × 36½″ (7.6cm × 92.7cm)	3½″ × 62½″ (8.9cm × 158.8cm)	4″ × 88½″ (10.2cm × 224.8cm)	4½″ × 88″ (11.4cm × 227.3cm)	5″ × 103″ (12.7cm × 261.6cm)
Long mitered border—cut 2	3″ × 49″ (7.6cm × 124.5cm)	3½″ × 87½″ (8.9cm × 222.3cm)	4″ × 88½″ (10.2cm × 224.8cm)	4½″ × 101″ (11.4cm × 259.1cm)	5″ × 103″ (12.7cm × 261.6cm)
Total fabric needed	1½ yds (1.37m)	4 yds (3.66m)	7 yds (6.4m)	7½ yds (6.86m)	8½ yds (7.77m)

Contrast Fabric

	BABY	TWIN	DOUBLE	QUEEN	KING
Short border—cut 2	1″ × 26″ (2.5cm × 66cm)	1″ × 51″ (2.5cm × 129.5cm)	1″ × 77″ (2.5cm × 195.6cm)	1″ × 77″ (2.5cm × 195.6cm)	1″ × 88″ (2.5cm × 223.5cm)
Long border—cut 2	1″ × 39 (2.5cm × 99.1cm)	1″ × 76″ (2.5cm × 193cm)	1″ × 76″ (2.5cm × 193cm)	1″ × 89″ (2.5cm × 226.1cm)	1″ × 89″ (2.5cm × 226.1cm)
Short sashing strips—1″ × 13″ (2.5cm × 33cm)	4	20	30	36	42
Long sashing strips	1 1″ × 38″ (2.5cm × 96.5cm)	3 1″ × 76″ (2.5cm × 193cm)	5 1″ × 76″ (2.5cm × 193cm)	5 1″ × 88″ (2.5cm × 223.5cm)	6 1″ × 88″ (2.5cm × 223.5cm)
Binding—2½″ (6.4cm) wide	170″ (4.32m)	300″ (7.6m)	355″ (9.01m)	380″ (9.65m)	410″ (10.4m)
Total fabric needed	1¼ yds (1.14m)	2½ yds (2.06m)	2½ yds (2.06m)	3 yds (2.74m)	3 yds (2.74m)

	BABY	TWIN	DOUBLE	QUEEN	KING
Backing	1½ yds (1.37m)	5 yds (4.57m)	5 yds (4.57m)	6 yds (5.49m)	8½ yds (7.77m)
Fusible interfacing	1 yd (.91m)	2 yds (1.83)	2¾ yds (2.51m)	3¼ yds (2.97m)	3½ yds (3.2m)

Cutting

1. Using templates A and E and following the charts above, cut out the required number of pieces from the tie fabric. Freezer-paper templates (page xv) are recommended for this project. First cut all the diamonds for the swallows (template A), 24 for each block, then use the leftover fabric to cut triangles for the sawtooth border (template E).

2. Cut the outside border pieces parallel to the selvages on the background fabric. Press and cut all other templates according to the requirements in the charts above. Stack or store these pieces with the appropriate diamond tie pieces by block.

3. Cut the binding strips from the contrast fabric parallel to the selvage. Measure and cut the remaining pieces, beginning with the longest and finishing with the shortest.

Making the Quilt Top

This pattern may be sewn by machine, or by hand using the English paper piecing method (page xv).

1. Lay out the large diamonds (three template As and four template Bs) following Diagram 1.

2. Pin and sew each large diamond following the order indicated in Diagram 2. Sew piece 1 to piece 2 from edge to edge. Sew piece 3 to piece 4 from the first pin off the opposite edge (see Diagram 3). Press all seams. Pin and sew piece 2 to piece 3 as above, piece 4 to piece 5, and

It is very important that all seams be exactly the same size, since even the smallest variation can alter the entire quilt size. When placing the large diamonds, make certain the pattern on each piece is facing the right way so the swallows fly in the same direction.

Diagram 1

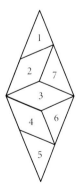

Diagram 2

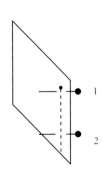

Diagram 3

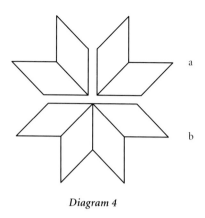

Diagram 4

⌇ *These instructions are for a baby quilt. If your quilt is larger, attach additional rows in the same manner.*

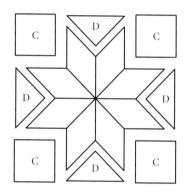

Diagram 5

Row 1   Row 2

Diagram 6

piece 6 to piece 7. Press. Repeat until you have eight large pieced diamonds for each block.

3. For each block, pin and sew eight large diamonds into four pairs (see Diagram 4a) and press. *Do not* sew into the seam allowance at the outside edge. Join two pairs to form half a star (see Diagram 4b) and press. Again, do not sew into the seam allowance. Pin both star halves together to make a whole, and sew from seam allowance to seam allowance, matching the center seams exactly. Press.

4. Set in the outside triangles (template D) and squares (template C), as shown in Diagram 5. Press the seams away from the center star, being careful not to stretch the block. Repeat for each block.

5. Lay out your blocks and place the short and long sashing pieces where they belong (see Diagram 6). Sew a short sashing strip to the bottom of blocks 1, 2, 4, and 5. Connect all blocks and short sashing strips to form two rows. Press the seams toward the sashing. Attach Rows 1 and 2 with a long sashing strip between and press.

Making the Border

1. Lay out the background and tie triangles (template E) for the sawtooth border, placing the tie fabric toward the outside (see Diagram 7). Sew in pairs of alternating triangles (one background, one tie), and press seams toward the darker color. Using the table below as a guide, sew the pairs into fours, then eights, and so on, until your border is the correct length for each side of your quilt.

Number of triangles needed

	TIE FABRIC	BACKGROUND FABRIC
Baby	2 rows of 14	2 rows of 13
	2 rows of 21	2 rows of 20
Twin	2 rows of 28	2 rows of 27
	2 rows of 42	2 rows of 41
Double	2 rows of 43	2 rows of 42
	2 rows of 50	2 rows of 49
Queen	4 rows of 50	4 rows of 49
King	4 rows of 58	4 rows of 57

2. Pin and sew first the short, then the long, ½″ (1.3cm) border—which matches the sashing—around the quilt, being careful not to stretch the fabric.

3. Attach the light side of the sawtooth border to the top and bottom, then to the sides, from seam allowance to seam allowance.

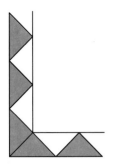

Diagram 7

4. Sew on the short outside borders, then the long ones, mitering the corners (see page xvi).

Quilting

Prepare your quilt for quilting by adding the backing and batting, following the instructions on page xix. There are many ways to quilt this pattern, but one of the prettiest is shown in Diagram 8.

1. Quilt in the ditch (seam line) around each block, diamond, and swallow; on each side of the sawtooth border; and between each triangle in the sawtooth border.
2. Quilt ¼″ (64mm) inside the seam line on the swallows to make them stand out.
3. Quilt ¼″ (64mm) from the edge of the large triangles and inside the seam allowances of the tie triangles in the sawtooth border.
4. Quilt each corner square from corner to corner.

Finishing the Quilt

Finish the edges of the quilt following the guidelines on page xix. Quilt the outer border with straight lines spaced ½″ (1.3cm) apart or use a feather design. Make and sew on the binding following the instructions on page xix. Use the same fabric for the binding as you used for the sashing. Since there is so much background color, a ½″ (1.3cm) binding is recommended.

Variations

If you are making a baby quilt, you might want to try making each block from a different pastel tie.

Enjoy your flying swallows with their peaceful swirling motion.

Diagram 8

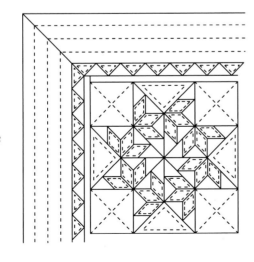

Grandmother's Flower Garden

28″ × 43¾″ (71cm × 111cm)

This scalloped-edge quilt uses ties of soft blues and browns for the flowers, set together with a cream garden path. It is finished with a powder blue binding.

Grandmother's Flower Garden

$\mathcal{F}$lower garden quilts originated in twelfth-century England, where tiny hexagons were sewn into designs of flowers and borders. Brought to America by English settlers, GRANDMOTHER'S FLOWER GARDEN was often used to teach young girls how to sew. The overall pattern of hexagons, or "sixes," is strongly associated with the quilt revival of the 1930s, when pastels replaced bright colors to give a lighter, happier look to Depression-era quilts.

Because the pattern uses only one shape, it can be adapted to any size quilt, with hexagon shapes ranging from ⅝″ (1.6cm) to 5″ (12.7cm). When made by English paper piecing, the hexagons match perfectly.

Choosing Fabrics

Look at live flowers for inspiration—bright orange-red poppies, blue-purple lupins, or velvety irises in a variety of hues. Choose ties with brilliant colors and shimmery finishes to give a jewel-like appearance and crisp sharp edges to the hexagons. Tie fabrics may blend or contrast, but they should be lightweight. You will need a single background fabric for the garden path that makes the flowers stand out, and binding in a color that blends with the tie fabric.

Block Construction

The finished size of the quilt includes a narrow binding. Use the chart below to determine how many blocks you will need.

	BABY 28″ × 43¾″ (71.1cm × 111.1cm)	TWIN 64″ × 91″ (162.6cm × 231.1cm)	DOUBLE 73″ × 91″ (185.4cm × 231.1cm)	QUEEN 82″ × 91″ (208.2cm × 231.1cm)	KING 100″ × 106I″ (254cm × 271.1cm)
Number of odd rows	3	6	6	6	7
Flowers in each odd row	3	7	8	9	11
Number of even rows	2	5	5	5	6
Flowers in each even row	2	6	7	8	10
Total number of flowers	13	72	83	94	137

Fabric Requirements

The quilt shown uses all blue and brown ties for the flowers, alternating the colors between Ring 1 and Ring 2 of each flower. A mixture of brown ties with a blue design and blue ties with a brown design in addition to some solids provides balance. The garden path is in a cream background fabric.

All of the flowers are made from tie fabric. You may also make the flower centers from tie fabric, as in the quilt shown here, or from background fabric. A nice touch is to use yellow fabric for the flower centers. If you choose to use this instead of tie or background fabric, follow the amounts given in the last table below.

Tie Fabric ⮑ *Number of templates needed*

	BABY	TWIN	DOUBLE	QUEEN	KING
Hexagons per flower *(template A)*	19	19	19	19	19
Total flower hexagons	247	1,368	1,577	1,786	2,603

Background Fabric

	BABY	TWIN	DOUBLE	QUEEN	KING
Garden path hexagons *(template A)*	150	682	776	870	1,238
Total fabric needed	1 yd (.91m)	2¾ yds (2.51m)	3¼ yds (2.97m)	3¼ yds (2,97m)	5 yds (4.57m)

Other

	BABY	TWIN	DOUBLE	QUEEN	KING
Yellow fabric for flower centers	⅛ yd (.11m)	½ yd (.46m)	½ yd (.46m)	⅝ yd (.57m)	¾ yd (.69m)
Bias binding—1¾″ (4.4cm) wide	1¼ yds (1.1m)	1¾ yds (1.6m)	1¾ yds (1.6m)	1¾ yds (1.6m)	2 yds (1.8m)
Backing	1½ yds (1.37m)	5½ yds (5m)	5½ yds (5m)	5½ yds (5m)	9¼ yds (8.4m)

~ If the tie is wide and has an overall design (or is solid), it should yield about 46 hexagons. You will need more ties when there is a design that must be centered in each hexagon.

Cutting

1. Using template A and following the charts above, cut out the required number of pieces from the tie fabric. Make sure there is enough fabric for six or twelve matching hexagons (one complete flower ring). Freezer-paper templates (page xv) are recommended for this project. Keep one edge of the hexagon consistently on the straight grain—either crosswise or lengthwise. If the fabric has a stripe or flower design, this should take priority over the grain. Cut all the hexagons ¼″ (64mm) from the template edge.

2. If you are using a tie with a design that should be centered in each hexagon, use the window template (template B). Place the tie right side up and position the template so the design you want appears in the window. Press template A in the opening. Repeat as needed, leaving ¼″ (64mm) around each template. Cut and store all pieces for each flower separately.

3. Cut the hexagons from background fabric and the bias binding according to the requirements given in the tables above. Cut flower centers from whichever fabric you choose.

Making the Quilt Top

1. Baste under the seam allowances for all flower hexagons. Press and store separately as before.

2. For each flower, lay out basted hexagons in two rings around a center. Arrange fabric designs as desired. Hold the center hexagon and one hexagon from the first ring with right sides facing. Whip stitch one side (see Diagram 1). Open and finger press (see Diagram 2).

3. Continue adding flower hexagons around the center, sewing connecting seams as you go (see Diagram 3). Add the second circle of hexagons in the same manner (see Diagram 4). Press lightly. Repeat for all flowers in the quilt.

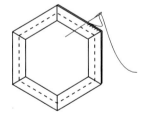

Diagram 1

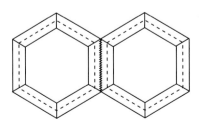

Diagram 2

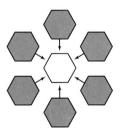

Diagram 3

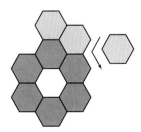

Diagram 4

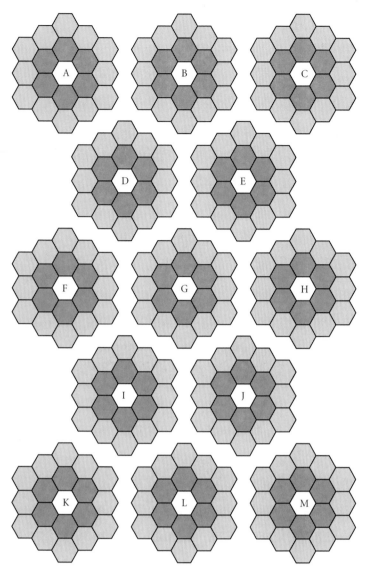

Diagram 5

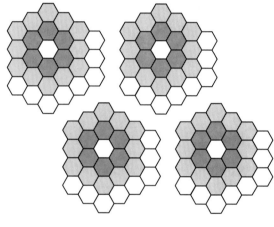

Diagram 6

4. Place the completed flowers on a white sheet with the width of a garden path between them. Arrange as desired, placing similar flowers in different areas for a scrap effect. Working across the top row, label each flower A, B, C, and so on, from left to right (see Diagram 5). Repeat for each row. Store or stack the flowers by rows.

5. Sew eight background hexagons to each flower (see Diagram 6). Press. Sew the flowers for Row 1 together in sequence, keeping the path between them and making sure the center hexagon of each flower is turned with a straight edge at the top. Attach the flowers in Row 2 to Row 1 in the same way. Continue until all rows have been connected.

6. Add extra background hexagons around the outside of the quilt as needed. The flowers should be completely surrounded by the garden path. Press.

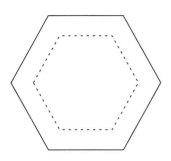

Diagram 7

Making the Border

This quilt does not have a separate border. A scalloped edge results from the sides of the hexagons.

Quilting

Prepare your quilt for quilting by adding the backing and batting, following the instructions on page xix. Outline quilt ¼″ (64mm) from the edge of all hexagons (see Diagram 7).

Finishing the Quilt

Finish the edge of the quilt following the guidelines on page xix. Quilt the border as desired. Make and sew on the binding following the instructions on page xix.

Variations

I prefer a scalloped edge on this quilt, but you can create a straight edge on the sides if you wish.

1. Fill in around the side edges with half flowers.
2. Cut a straight line down the sides and bind as usual.

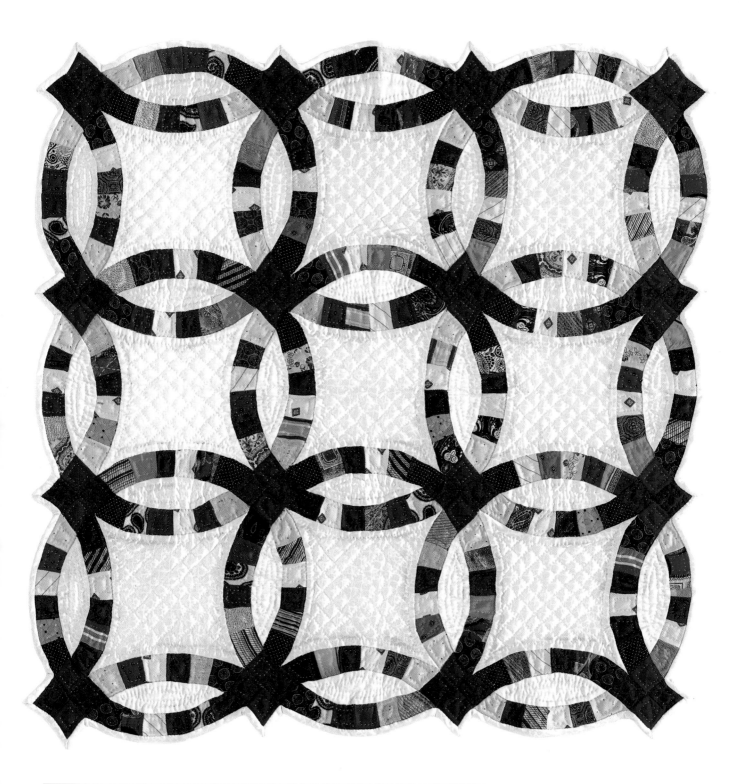

Double Wedding Ring

28″ × 28″ (71cm × 71cm)

This small quilt or wall hanging is made in exactly the same way as a larger quilt. On a white background, the jewel-like multi-colored rings are made from ties. The points where the rings meet are made of the same two colors throughout the quilt.

Double Wedding Ring

*L*ittle is known about the origins of this romantic pattern, which has become the embodiment of American patchwork, but by the 1920s it was one of the most beloved patterns in the country. Often made as a gift for weddings and special anniversaries, DOUBLE WEDDING RING is said to symbolize love and marriage. The many colors used in DOUBLE WEDDING RING are also thought to parallel the rich tapestry of married life. In fact, these family heirlooms dating back to the Depression era were often made from multi-color fabric scraps from children's clothes.

Known variously as The Rainbow, Around the World, King Tut, and Endless Chain, this pattern is tough for a beginner. For the experienced quilter, any number of rings can be connected to make any size quilt.

Choosing Fabrics

You need to decide on your background color for this quilt first. If you choose a light color, as I did, almost any tie may be used for the arc pieces. If you prefer a dark background, lighter-color ties are a better choice. No matter what color ties you use, those with shiny surfaces work much better in this quilt than those with matte finishes as bright, clear colors give a jewel-like effect against a light background, and softer colors highlight more dramatically on a dark background.

Block Construction

This pattern is made up of five templates, four of which make up the units in each block (see Diagram 1). Template A is used for the four center pieces of each arc. Templates B and BR are slightly different in shape and are sewn to each end of the arcs, B on one end and BR on the other. Template C is the connecting piece between the arcs. Half of the C templates are cut from one color and half from a contrasting color. Templates D and E are cut from background fabric.

Use the chart below to determine how many blocks you will need.

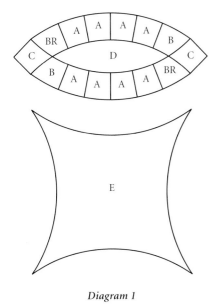

Diagram 1

	TWIN 61½″ × 78″ (156.2cm × 198.1cm)	DOUBLE 78 × 86¼″ (198.1cm × 219.1cm)	QUEEN 86¼″ × 94½″ (219.1cm × 240cm)	KING 94½″ × 94½″ (240cm × 240cm)
Full blocks	32	45	55	61
Partial blocks #1	14	15	17	20
Extra centers	17	28	36	40
Partial blocks #2	0	2	2	0
Units in quilt *(see Diagram 2)*	142	199	241	264

⤳ The block size is 12″ × 12″ (30.5cm), but because the rings overlap, each ring after the first adds only 8¼″ (21cm).

Fabric Requirements

The number and type of template pieces you need for your quilt will depend on the size of your quilt (see Diagram 2). Only a tie fabric and a background fabric are required.

Tie Fabric ⤳ *Number of templates needed*

	TWIN	DOUBLE	QUEEN	KING
Arc pieces *(template A)*	1,136	1,592	1,928	2,112
Arc pieces *(template B)*	284	398	482	528
Arc pieces *(template BR)*	284	398	482	528
Connecting pieces *(template C)*	284	398	482	528

Background Fabric

	TWIN	DOUBLE	QUEEN	KING
Ellipses *(template D)*	142	199	241	264
Centers *(template E)*	63	90	110	121
Bias binding 1¾″ (4.5cm) wide	330″ 8.38m	390″ 9.91m	430″ 10.92m	470″ 11.94m
Total fabric needed	4½ yds (4.11m)	5½ yds (5.03m)	5¾ yds (5.26m)	6¾ yds (6.17m)

Other

	TWIN	DOUBLE	QUEEN	KING
Backing	5 yds (4.57m)	5¼ yds (4.8m)	8½ yds (7.77m)	8½ yds (7.77m)

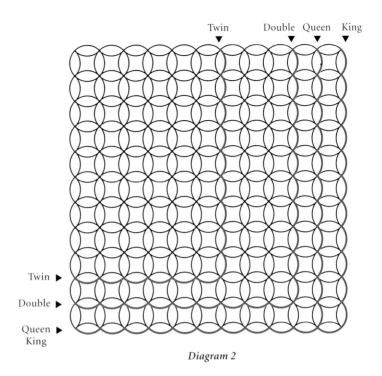

Diagram 2

Cutting

As you place the templates on the tie fabric, try to place one straight edge of each template on the straight grain to help you control the arcs—if they are cut on the bias, the fabric can stretch out of shape. If this is impossible, use freezer paper to prevent stretching.

1. Following the charts above, trace and cut freezer-paper templates (see page xv) for the required pieces of tie fabric. Remember to leave ¼″ (64mm) around all templates for seam allowances. Stack the pieces in groups by template or store them in separate, clearly labeled bags (be sure to keep templates B and BR separate).

2. First cut the bias binding from the background fabric, then cut the required number of pieces for templates D and E. Stack or store the pieces separately until ready to use.

Making the Quilt Top

Before pinning the pieces together lay out all of the arcs to better see where the colors should be placed.

1. Pin half of the arcs together as follows: BR to A, A to A, and A to B. Pin the other half of the arcs as B to A, A to A, and A to BR (see Diagram 3). Make sure that the pins are at the top and bottom of the freezer-paper pieces (see Diagram 4).

2. Make a light pencil mark (in the seam allowance or on the freezer paper) in the centers of each side of template D and on all four sides of template E (see Diagram 5).

3. Sew all of arc a from Diagram 3 first. Chain sew all of the pinned pieces (see page xv), then cut the long strip into groups of three. Pin these three sections together, and sew. Press all seams in the arc to the left. This will make attaching the arcs to the ellipse much easier.

4. Repeat this procedure for arc b.

5. Sew the two C templates to the ends of arc a, using a different color at each end (see Diagram 6).

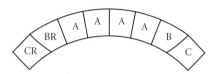

a

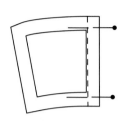

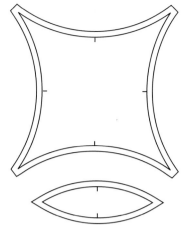

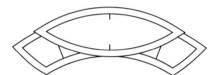

b

Diagram 3

Diagram 4

Diagram 5

Diagram 6

Diagram 7

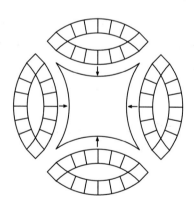

Diagram 8

〜 *If you prefer to hand sew the blocks:*

1. *Make the clips in the seam allowances of template E. Baste under and press.*

2. *Lay template E on top of the section seam allowance and pin. Hand sew in place.*

3. *Continue pinning and sewing all blocks to complete the quilt top.*

6. Lay arc b right side up. Pin the center mark of template D to the center seam line of arc b (see Diagram 7). Pin the right end of the ellipse to the right end of the arc at the seam allowance. Begin sewing at the edge, around the center, and off the opposite end. Be sure to keep template D on top when you sew.

7. Pin and sew arc a to the opposite side of the ellipse, matching seams as necessary, to form a complete section. Press. Complete all of the sections in the same manner.

8. Clip around template E, halfway into the seam allowance, every ½″ (1.3cm) to make sewing around the curves easier.

9. For each full block, lay out four sections around each template E (see Diagram 8). Attach one section to the side of template E using the method described above for attaching ellipses to arcs. Attach another section to the opposite side of the template and press. Repeat for the other two sides.

10. Follow the chart on page 76 to make the correct number of partial blocks #1 (a template E with one side section) and #2 (a template E with two side sections). There will be several template E pieces left for all quilt sizes.

11. Using Diagram 9 as a guide, draw a diagram for your quilt size and lay out the entire quilt, making sure the blocks are arranged the way you want them.

12. Pin and sew the blocks together for each row. Press the seams toward the center of each block. Pin and sew Rows 1 and 2 together, matching the points of the template E pieces to align the arcs. Repeat for each row. Press.

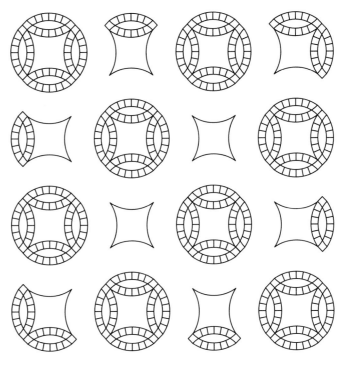

Diagram 9

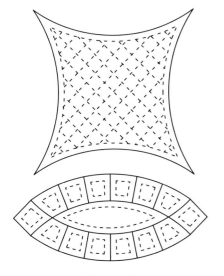

Diagram 10

Quilting

Prepare your quilt for quilting by adding the backing and batting, following the instructions on page xix.

The quilting in this pattern, as in the other patterns in this book, is very simple (see Diagram 10). However, you may use a more elaborate design in the centers of the blocks if you choose.

1. Quilt in the ditch (seam line) around the ellipses and the large ovals.
2. Quilt inside each arc piece and the ellipses.
3. Quilt the center of each block from point to point using parallel lines, ½″ (1.3cm) apart, in both directions.

Finishing the Quilt

Finish the edge of the quilt following the guidelines on page xix.

Variations

Following Diagram 1 and using shades of one color, make the two center A pieces the lightest, the A pieces on either side medium-shade, pieces B and BR dark. One of the C pieces can be in the darkest shade of all, with the other C piece in a contrast color.

Consider giving this lovely quilt as a gift to a special couple.

Sentimental Sampler

67″ × 83″ (170cm × 211cm)

Black and white blocks, borders, and binding set off blocks from each pattern in this book. Each pattern block is made with a variety of tie fabrics.

Sentimental Sampler

SENTIMENTAL SAMPLER comprises sixteen 12″ × 12″ (30.5cm) blocks and two double blocks for Grandmother's Flower Garden and Double Wedding Ring patterns. Two Nosegay blocks are at the center of the quilt, while four Grandmother's Fan blocks are placed at the corners. There are also variations of two patterns—a Sunflower block (a variation on Dresden Plate) and an Eight-Pointed Star block (a variation on Flying Swallows).

This sampler is a good way to learn how to make and experiment with many different designs. It can also help you decide which patterns you would like to use for an entire quilt.

Choosing Fabrics

First, choose a color scheme for the quilt as a whole, then pick out all the ties you have in that color scheme. The quilt may be made from four or five colors, or it can be a scrap quilt of many colors. Divide the ties by quilt blocks, keeping in mind that some ties will be used in several blocks. When you begin cutting, work on the blocks that use large pieces first. You can then cut smaller pieces from the leftover fabric as needed.

For simplicity, I recommend using a white or cream fabric for the background and sashing, with a second contrasting color for the binding and the narrow frames around each block.

Block Construction

The sampler shown in Diagram 1 is 67″ × 83″ (170cm × 211cm) and may be used on either a twin or a double bed. It includes a ½″ (1.3cm) frame strip around each block and 3″ (7.6cm) sashing and posts. It can be enlarged by adding a 4″ (10.2cm), 6″ (15.2cm), or 8″ (20.3cm) border or by using two regular borders. Alternatively, the sashing may be made 1″ (2.5cm) wider— that is 4″ (10.2cm).

You will need 16 blocks of 12″ × 12″ (30.5cm) and 2 blocks of 12″ × 27″ (30.5cm × 68.6cm).

Grandmother's Fan	4
Dresden Plate	1
Seven Sisters	1
Wild Goose Chase	1
Grandmother's Flower Garden	1 double block of three flowers
Spools	1
Dahlia	1
Nosegay	2
Flying Swallows	1
Milky Way	1
Double Wedding Ring	1 double block of three rings
Ocean Waves	1
Eight-Pointed Star	1
Sunflower	1

Diagram 1

Fabric Requirements

You will need ties for all blocks and a background fabric for the blocks, sashing, and matching sashing border. A contrast fabric is used for block frames, connecting sashing squares and a binding. The following table gives an overview of how many templates you will need for each pattern. Unless otherwise noted, one block is made from each pattern.

Number of templates needed

Grandmother's Fan (4 blocks)	
Fan blade (template A)	32 (4 sets of 8 different blades)
Fan handle (template B)	4
Dresden Plate	
Plate wedge (template A)	16
Plate center (template B)	1
Seven Sisters	
Star diamonds (template A)	42
Background diamonds (template C)	12
Wild Goose Chase	
Large triangle (template A)	4
Center square (template B)	1
Corner square (template C)	4
Goose triangle (template D)	8
Small triangle (template E)	24
Grandmother's Flower Garden (1 double block)	
Hexagon (template A)	57
center	3 (1 for each flower)
first ring	18 (6 for each flower)
second ring	36 (12 for each flower)
Spools	
Trapezoid (template A)	16
spool end	8
background	8
Thread (template B)	4
Dahlia	
Flower petal (template A)	6
Flower center (template B)	1
Nosegay (2 blocks)	
Flower holder (template A)	2
Flower petal (template B)	12
Background (templates C and CR)	2 of each
Flower center (template D)	10
Background (template E and ER)	6 of each
Background (template F)	8
Flying Swallows*	
Swallow (template A)	24

Background *(template B)*	32
Background *(template C)*	4
Background *(template D)*	4

Milky Way

Center square *(template A)*	1
Four-patch *(template B)*	
Tie	8
Background	8
Large triangle *(template C)*	8
Tie	4
Background	4

Double Wedding Ring (1 double block)

Arc piece *(template A)*	80
End piece of arc *(templates B and BR)*	20
Connecting piece *(template C)*	20
Background *(template D)*	10
Background *(template E)*	3

Ocean Waves

Waves *(template A)*	
Tie	48
Background	48
Center *(template B)*	1
Corner triangle *(template D)*	4

Eight-Pointed Star

Background *(template C from Flying Swallows)*	4
Background *(template D from Flying Swallows)*	4
Large star diamond *(template A this chapter)*	8

Sunflower

Center *(template B from Dresden Plate)*	1
Pointed wedge *(template B this chapter)*	16

You will need additional fabric for the background, sashing, and a sashing border. A contrast fabric is used for a narrow frame around the blocks, the sashing squares, and the binding.

Background fabric	5 yds
	4.57m
Contrast fabric	2½ yds
	2.29m
Backing (cotton fabric)	5 yds
	4.57m

~ *As you lay out and cut the tie pieces for each block, store them in a zipper bag. This will keep them organized and save time when you begin assembling the blocks.*

Cutting

Using the templates from each of the chapters, templates A and B on page 101, and the chart above, cut out the required pieces of tie fabric for each block. Freezer-paper templates (page xv) are recommended for this project because of the number of pieces involved. Laying out all of the pieces ahead of time will help you avoid wasted fabric.

1. For tie-fabric pieces, press on freezer-paper templates for the blocks that require many pieces from one tie. When all the templates have been pressed on, cut out the pieces, leaving ¼″ (64mm) around each. Lay out the blocks that have the larger pieces first.

2. Cut background-fabric and contrast-fabric pieces as listed in the charts above.

Making the Quilt Top

1. Make one block at a time, following the directions in each chapter. Take the chapters in order, and make any variations on these patterns directly after you finish the originals. For example, make the Sunflower block right after the Dresden Plate block, using the same instructions but pointed wedges instead of rounded ones. The Eight-Pointed Star block should be made directly after the Flying Swallows block.

2. For Grandmother's Flower Garden, make the three flowers and appliqué them to one of the double background blocks, leaving the width of a garden path between each flower. Cut the background fabric from under each flower.

3. For Double Wedding Ring, make the three connected rings, including the centers and ellipses. Appliqué the rings to the center of the second double background block. Cut the background fabric from under the rings.

4. Lay out the blocks as outlined in Diagram 1. Sew a block frame strip to the sides of each block, and press seams toward the frame.

5. Sew a block frame strip to the top and bottom of each block using the four long strips at the top and bottom of the Flower Garden and Double Wedding Ring blocks.

6. Sew the sashing strips between the blocks in each horizontal row and on the outside of each row.

7. Connect the six horizontal sashing rows of squares and strips. Lay out the sashing rows and the quilt-block rows as shown in Diagram 1. Pin all intersection points of the top sashing strip to Row 1, and sew. Repeat for each row until you have completed the quilt top. Press seams toward the sashing strips.

Diagram 2

Quilting

Prepare your quilt for quilting by adding the backing and batting, following the instructions on page xix.

1. For the individual blocks, follow the directions in each chapter or quilt as you wish.

2. Quilt in the ditch (seam line) around the narrow frames.

3. Quilt the sashing strips in diagonal lines ½″ (1.3cm) apart in both directions. Quilt the sashing squares with diagonal lines from corner to corner, then with a smaller triangle in each produced by these two lines (see Diagram 2).

Finishing the Quilt

Finish the edge of the quilt following the guidelines on page xix. Quilt the border as desired. Make and sew on the binding following the instructions on page xix.

As you enjoy your quilt, decide which block is your favorite, dig into your tie collection, and start your next project.

TEMPLATES
&
LESSON
PLAN

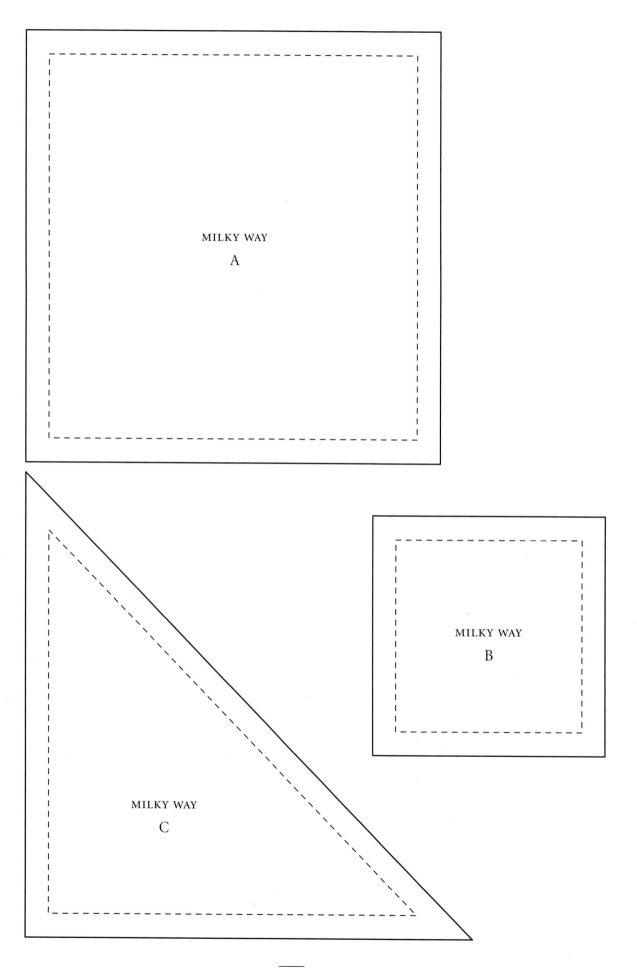

MILKY WAY

A

MILKY WAY

B

MILKY WAY

C

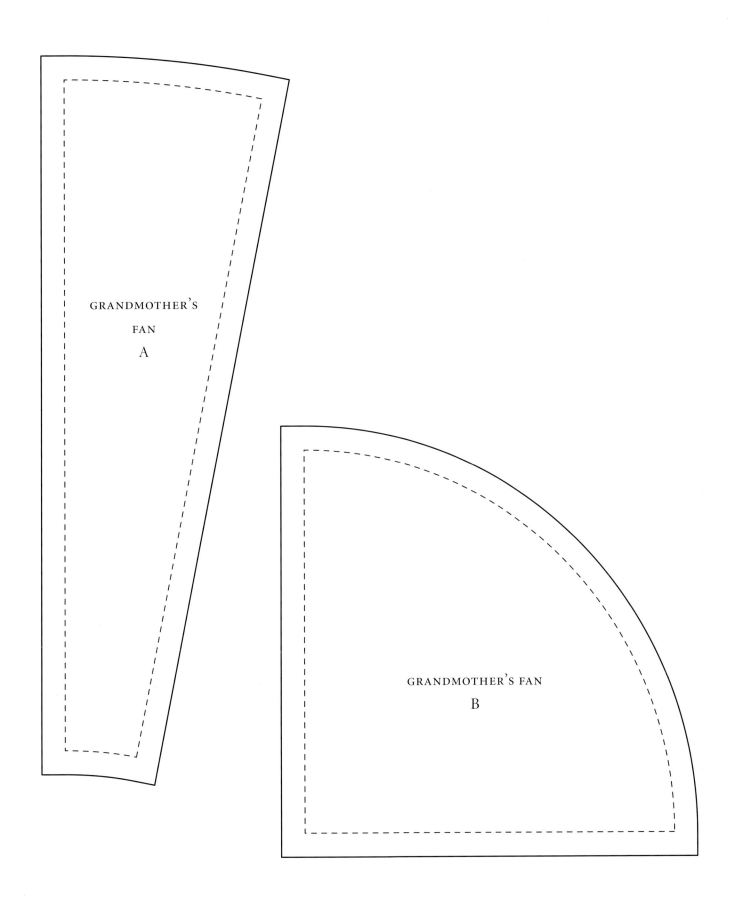

GRANDMOTHER'S
FAN
A

GRANDMOTHER'S FAN
B

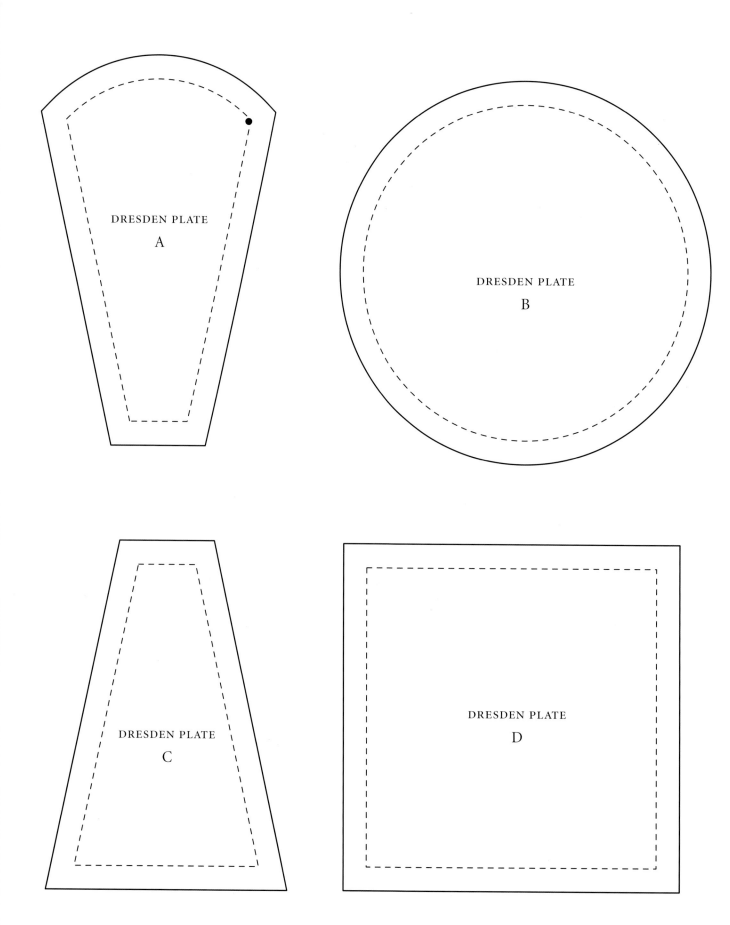

DRESDEN PLATE
A

DRESDEN PLATE
B

DRESDEN PLATE
C

DRESDEN PLATE
D

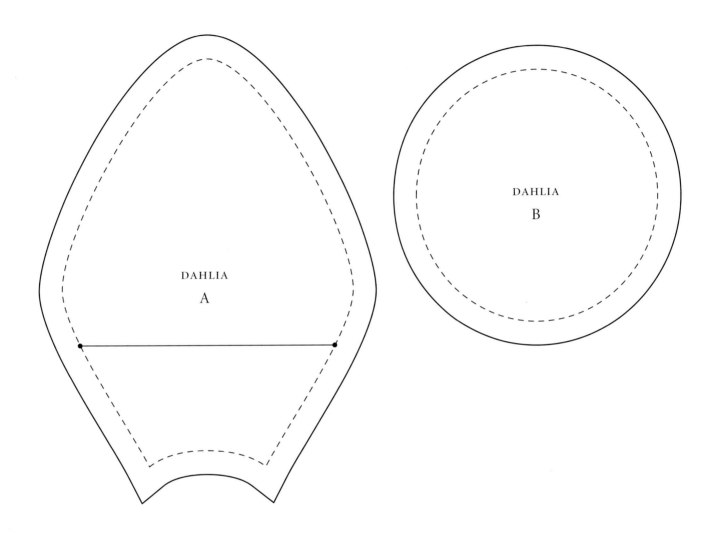

DAHLIA

A

DAHLIA

B

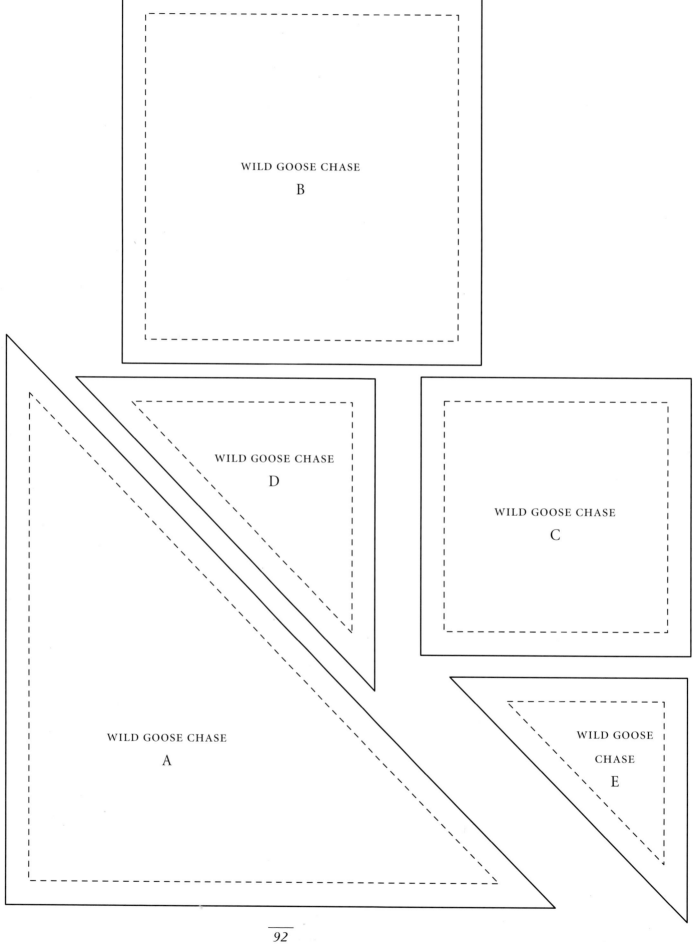

WILD GOOSE CHASE

B

WILD GOOSE CHASE

D

WILD GOOSE CHASE

C

WILD GOOSE CHASE

A

WILD GOOSE CHASE

E

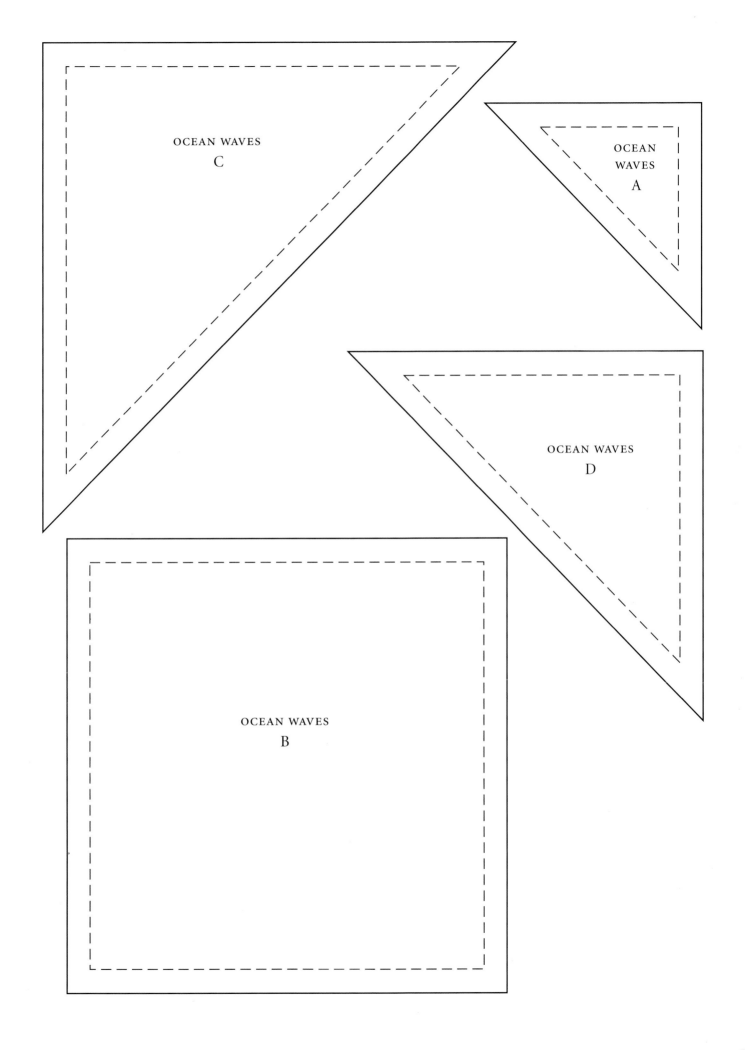

OCEAN WAVES
C

OCEAN
WAVES
A

OCEAN WAVES
D

OCEAN WAVES
B

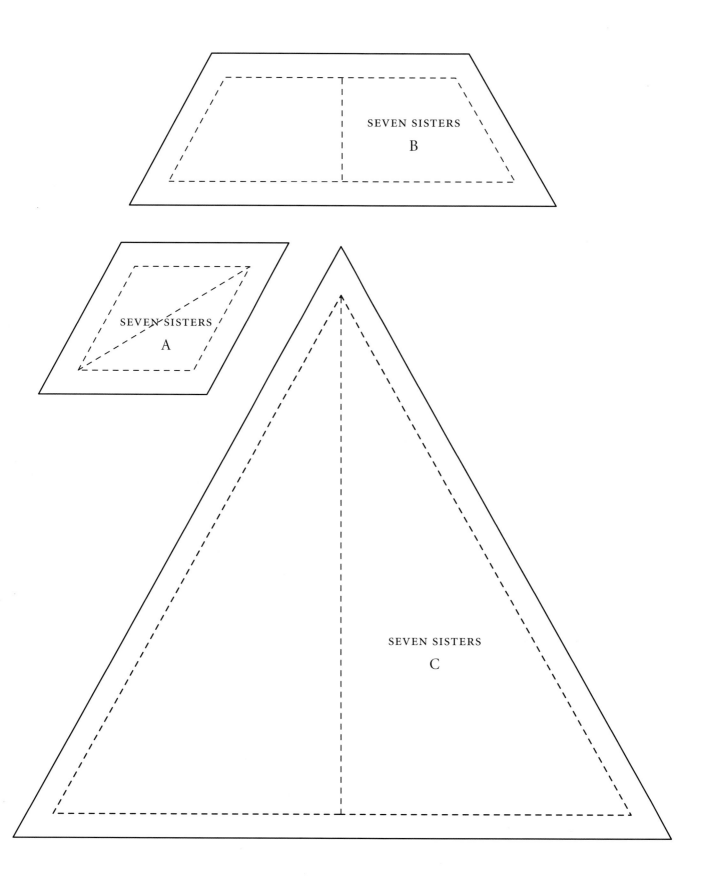

SEVEN SISTERS
B

SEVEN SISTERS
A

SEVEN SISTERS
C

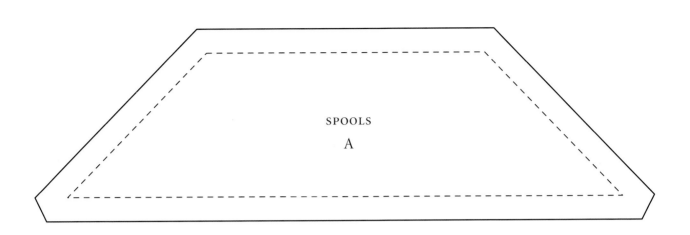

SPOOLS

A

SPOOLS

B

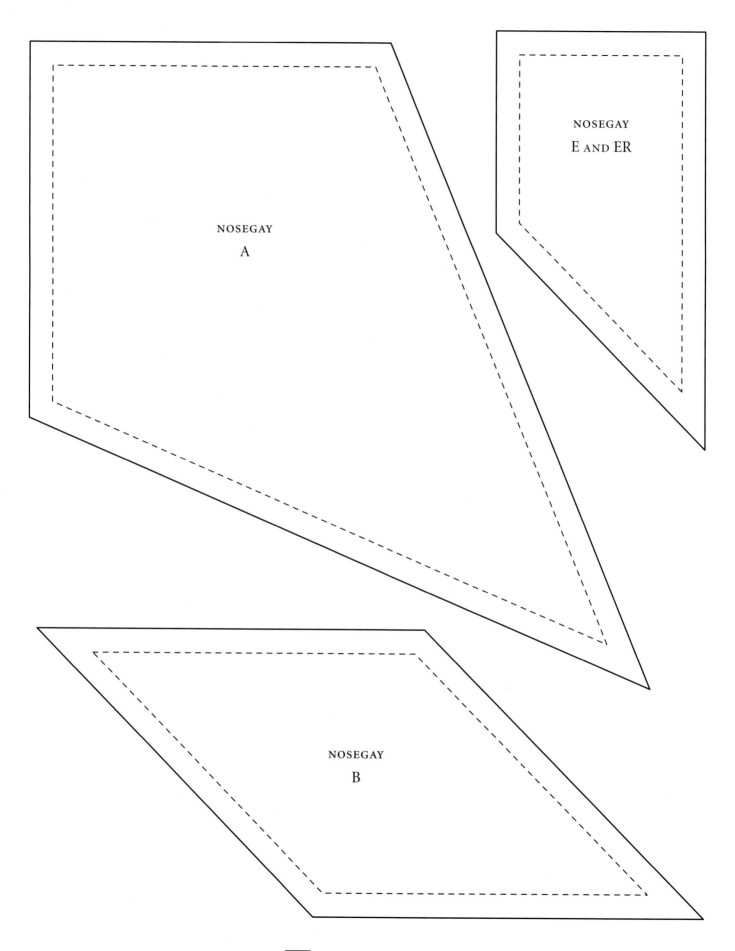

NOSEGAY

A

NOSEGAY

E and ER

NOSEGAY

B

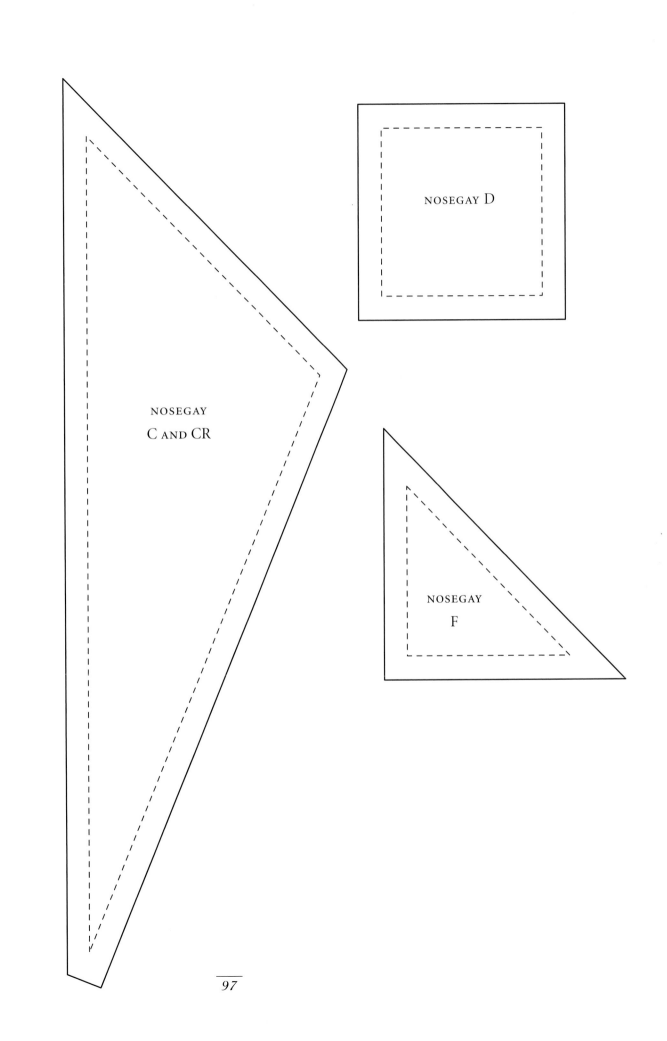

NOSEGAY D

NOSEGAY
C AND CR

NOSEGAY
F

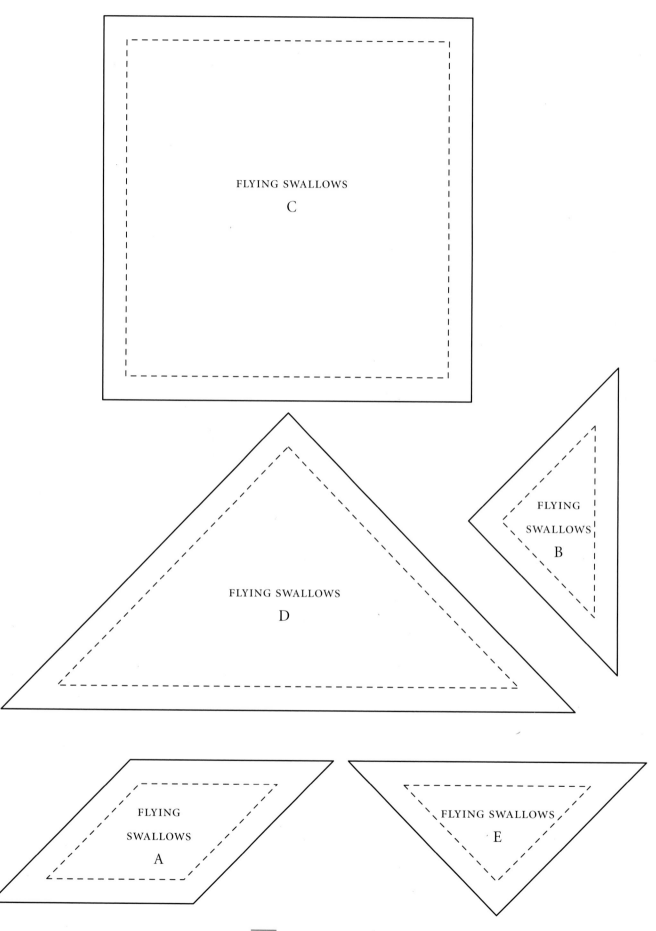

FLYING SWALLOWS
C

FLYING SWALLOWS
D

FLYING
SWALLOWS
B

FLYING
SWALLOWS
A

FLYING SWALLOWS
E

GRANDMOTHER'S

FLOWER

GARDEN

A

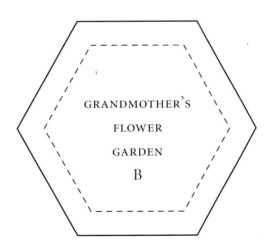

GRANDMOTHER'S

FLOWER

GARDEN

B

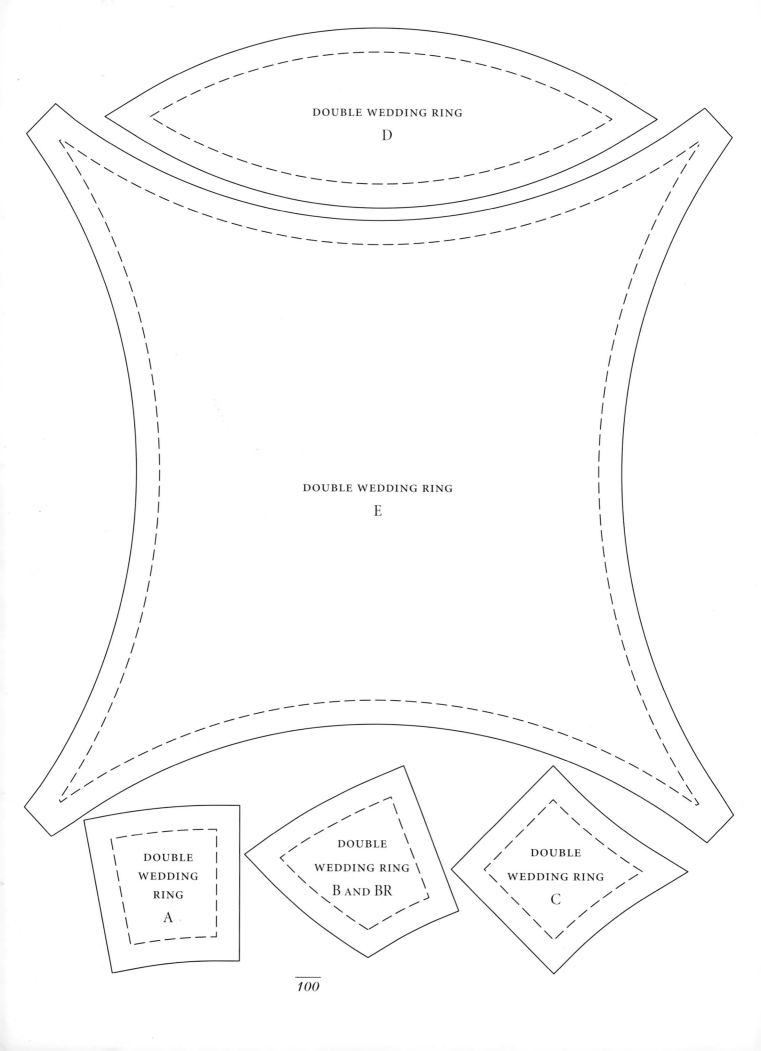

DOUBLE WEDDING RING

D

DOUBLE WEDDING RING

E

DOUBLE
WEDDING
RING

A

DOUBLE
WEDDING RING

B AND BR

DOUBLE
WEDDING RING

C

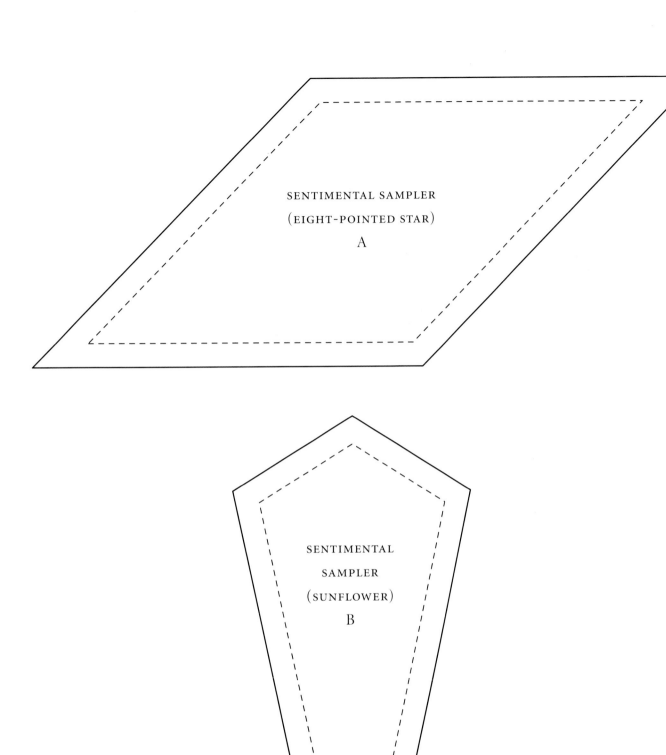

SENTIMENTAL SAMPLER
(EIGHT-POINTED STAR)
A

SENTIMENTAL
SAMPLER
(SUNFLOWER)
B

Lesson Plan

General Supplies

Threads & Ties That Bind

Shears

Paper scissors

Glass-head pins

Seam ripper

Thimble

Hand sewing needles

Notebook

Pencil

Additional Supplies

One tie

12″ (30cm) ruler

Freezer paper

Template plastic

This eight-week classroom schedule works well for the beginning quilter, teaching the basics of quilt making while introducing exquisite tie fabrics. Based around GRANDMOTHER'S FAN, the lessons cover essential techniques in a sequential system, from creating blocks and quilt tops to adding borders, sashings, and bindings. The schedule can be easily applied to any of the patterns in *Threads & Ties That Bind*.

Class One

Discuss

- Pleasures of quilt making
- Anatomy of a quilt
- Equipment and supplies
- Choosing a color plan
- Using tie fabrics
- Choosing and preparing ties
- Using freezer-paper templates

Demonstrate

- Preparing ties
- Making a master template
- Making and using freezer-paper templates

Participation

- Decide quilt size
- Draw a quilt diagram
- Take a tie apart
- Make a master template
- Trace fan blades from GRANDMOTHER'S FAN onto freezer paper and cut

Homework

- Read chapter on GRANDMOTHER'S FAN
- Choose ties and prepare for use
- Complete cutting freezer-paper templates

Prepared ties

Freezer paper templates

Sewing machine

Neutral thread

Class Two

Demonstrate

- Using tie designs in fan blades
- Sewing blades together

Participation

- Press blade templates on ties and cut enough for one fan
- Make one fan
- Continue cutting fan blades

Homework

- Complete cutting fan blades
- Continue to make fans

Additional Supplies

Sheer interfacing

12″ x 12″ (30cm x 30cm) paper

Class Three

Demonstrate

- Making facings for the fans
- Attaching facings

Participation

- Cut a paper facing pattern
- Cut facings for fans
- Sew a facing to one fan
- Continue working on fans

Homework

- Complete cutting facings
- Continue to work on fans

Class Four

Discuss

- Choosing background/border and sashing fabric
- Choosing backing fabric

Participation

- Continue working on fans

Homework

- Purchase background/border, sashing, and backing fabric
- Complete the remaining fans

Class Five

Additional Supplies

Background fabric

Rotary cutter

Rotary cutting mat

Wide plastic ruler

12½″ x 12½″ (30cm x 30cm) plastic ruler

Matching thread

Demonstrate

- Cutting borders and background squares using a rotary cutter
- Cutting fan handles
- Appliquéing handles to fans and fans to background

Participation

- Cut borders, background squares, and handles
- Prepare and appliqué handles to fans
- Begin appliquéing fans to background

Homework

- Complete appliquéing fans to background

Class Six

Additional Supplies

Sashing fabric

Rotary cutter

Rotary cutting mat

Marking pencil for hand quilting

Sewing machine

Neutral thread

Demonstrate

- Cutting sashing and borders
- Order for sewing blocks together
- Attaching sashing to blocks
- Sewing on borders
- Preparing backing

Participation

- Cut sashing
- Decide setting for blocks and mark this on diagram
- Decide quilting design
- Begin sewing blocks together

Homework

- Sew blocks together
- Attach borders
- Mark quilting lines
- Prepare backing

Additional Supplies

Backing fabric

Masking tape

Cotton darning needle, #1

Cotton basting thread

Class Seven

Discuss

- Choosing batting

Demonstrate

- Layering quilt

Participation

- Working in small groups, help baste each others' quilts

Homework

- Read material on quilting GRANDMOTHER'S FAN on page 13.

Additional Supplies

Quilting frame or hoop

Quilting needles, #9 or #10

Quilting thread

Class Eight

Demonstrate

- Using quilting frames and hoops
- Quilting stitch

Participation

- Begin hand quilting

Homework

- Continue quilting

∿ Try to meet up again as a class about six weeks after the final session. Compare quilts and share ideas. This extra meeting encourages everyone to complete GRANDMOTHER'S FAN—and to begin a new quilt.